Everyday Practices of Tourism Mobilities

The practice of packing a bag is a situation where subtle, daily processes can attune us to the relationships and experiences formed in mobile situations. There has been great attention to mundane and material practices in tourism, yet the process of packing, which is integral to any journey, remains unexamined.

Everyday Practices of Tourism Mobilities: Packing a Bag expands on the foundational theories of tourist practices through a rich assortment of photographic documentation and interviews with tourists in hostelling accommodation. It presents the intricacies and relations emerging through packing and the connections to an array of actors entwined in both touristic and everyday experiences of movement. Using case studies in Iceland and Nepal, the book explores how idealised tourist destinations influence everyday actions. The disjuncture between mundane routines and the heightened immersive environments is conducive to tourists attuning to the entanglement of actors and experiences beyond individual expectations. The book traces these moments of collective experiences to reflect on the intersections of globalised mobility and everyday tourist practices.

The international scope of this highly original and intriguing book will appeal to a broad academic audience, including scholars of tourism, cultural and social geography, mobilities studies, and environmental humanities.

Kaya Barry is an Associate Lecturer at the School of Humanities, Languages, and Social Science, and member of the Griffith Centre for Social and Cultural Research at Griffith University, Australia. Her research interests include mobilities, tourism, creative arts practice, materiality, communication aesthetics, and environmental humanities.

Routledge Advances in Tourism and Anthropology
Series Edited by Dr Catherine Palmer and Dr Jo-Anne Lester

Dr Catherine Palmer
University of Brighton, UK C.A.Palmer@brighton.ac.uk
Dr Jo-Anne Lester
University of Brighton, UK J.Lester@brighton.ac.uk

To discuss any ideas for the series please contact Faye Leerink, Commissioning Editor: *faye.leerink@tandf.co.uk* or the Series Editors.

This series draws inspiration from anthropology's overarching aim to explore and better understand the human condition in all its fascinating diversity. It seeks to expand the intellectual landscape of anthropology and tourism in relation to how we understand the experience of being human, providing critical inquiry into the spaces, places, and lives in which tourism unfolds. Contributions to the series will consider how such spaces are embodied, imagined, constructed, experienced, memorialised, and contested. The series provides a forum for cutting edge research and innovative thinking from tourism, anthropology, and related disciplines such as philosophy, history, sociology, geography, cultural studies, architecture, the arts, and feminist studies.

For a full list of titles in this series, please visit www.routledge.com/Routledge-Advances-in-Tourism-and-Anthropology/book-series/RATA

Published

Tourism and Ethnodevelopment
Inclusion, Empowerment and Self-determination
Edited by Ismar Borges de Lima and Victor T. King

Everyday Practices of Tourism Mobilities
Packing a Bag
Kaya Barry

Forthcoming

Post-Humanitarian Slum Tourism
Informal Urbanism, Affect and Subalternity
Tore E. H. Holst

Tourism and Indigenous Heritage in Latin America
Casper Jacobsen

Everyday Practices of Tourism Mobilities

Packing a Bag

Kaya Barry

Routledge
Taylor & Francis Group

LONDON AND NEW YORK

First published 2018 by Routledge
2 Park Square, Milton Park, Abingdon, Oxon OX14 4RN

52 Vanderbilt Avenue, New York, NY 10017

First issued in paperback 2020

Routledge is an imprint of the Taylor & Francis Group, an informa business

British Library Cataloguing-in-Publication Data
A catalogue record for this book is available from the British Library

Library of Congress Cataloging-in-Publication Data
A catalog record for this book has been requested

ISBN 13: 978-0-367-67049-8 (pbk)
ISBN 13: 978-0-415-78845-8 (hbk)

Typeset in Times New Roman
by Apex CoVantage, LLC

Contents

Figures

Acknowledgements

Thank you to everyone who participated in this project who so kindly interacted with me, answered my questions, and showed me their practices of packing. It certainly was a pleasure to have so many shared experiences in the hostel dorm rooms, common areas, and out and about in the surreal landscapes of Iceland and Nepal.

I am particularly thankful to the wonderful and lively hostels that allowed me to conduct research: Sirra and the staff at Reykjavík Downtown and Reykjavík Loft in Iceland; Tashi and the staff at Alobar1000 in Kathmandu, Nepal; and JIM and the staff at Circus Hostel in Berlin, Germany. This project was also enabled by my time spent at SÍM artist residency in Reykjavík and at Dalvík hostel.

I owe a lot of thanks to Jondi Keane, who guided my research and creative explorations. This project would never have unfolded without your support. I also want to thank my colleagues and friends who spurred on this research, in particular: Elizabeth Burrows, Cathy Perazzo, Giles Field, Michele Lobo, Tristam Horn, Cameron Bishop, and Patrick West. I am grateful for the ongoing support of the Griffith Centre for Social and Cultural Research and the School of Humanities, Languages, and Social Science at Griffith University, in addition to the School of Communication and Creative Arts at Deakin University, where this project began. I am also very grateful to the Editorial staff at Routledge and the reviewers who gave valuable advice. Thank you to everyone in the scholarly and artistic communities who gave advice and support for this research at the many conferences, invited seminars, exhibitions, and workshops where I presented my ideas, practices, and findings.

A big thank you to my family: Mum, Dad, Alana, Nana, the Jedskis, and Mr Xander, for waiting so patiently for me to return home and unpack.

Parts of this book have been adapted from previously published material and are reused with permission:

Chapter 2

Barry, K. 2016. 'Packing as practice: Creative knowledges through material interactions', *Tourism Analysis*, vol. 21, no. 4, pp. 403–416. doi: 10.3727/108354216X 14600320851776
Permission granted from Cognizant Communication Corporation.

Chapter 4

Barry, K. 2016. 'Transiting with the environment: An exploration of tourist re-orientations as collaborative practice', *Journal of Consumer Culture*, vol. 16, no. 2, pp. 374–392. doi: 10.1177/1469540516635406
Permission granted from SAGE Publications.

1   Introducing the Array of Actors

During a backpacking trip around Europe, a friend and I decided to visit Iceland. It was at the height of the Eyjafjallajökull eruption that halted global aviation. Getting to Iceland was a challenge in itself, as most flights were cancelled or delayed due to the volcanic ash cloud. After waiting all day in London Gatwick airport, ironically our flight to Iceland was one of the few flights out of the country that day.

One of the first things we did upon arrival in Iceland was book a tour to see the erupting volcano 'up close'. We left Reykjavík, the capital city, in a big tour truck at dusk, driving through the ash-covered landscape and streams of glacial meltwater. We were dropped off about three kilometres from the base of the small volcano. Ash filled the sky and our vision (Figure 1.1). Sounds rumbled below the ground, the air was thick with an earthly smell, and we had to wear a thin facemask. It was the epitome of an immersive environmental tourist experience.

We returned to our hostel dormitory room in the early hours of morning covered in ash. A person in the bunk bed next to me asked in a sleepy voice, 'what's that smell?' It was the earthly, ashy aroma that clung to our clothes. I dumped my clothes and boots that I had worn on the tour on top of my bag. The next morning all around my bag was covered in ash. Weeks later, we were still finding unexpected residue and pockets of ash in our clothes, and a fine dust would spill out of our bags while we were packing. It was an experience that infused the everyday, mundane process of packing a bag with the surreal, eruptive, earthly tourism experience.

In this instance, my friend and I, our bags, and the volcano became bound together. The interaction of materials, the spatial distribution of the ash, our bodies, bags, the ongoing process of movement and travel, and, perhaps most importantly, the resistance of the nonhuman actors involved—the ash residue and its relationship to the global travel event (Birtchnell and Büscher 2011)—all contributed to the complexity of the packing process and the relational, affective mobilities involved. This experience in tourism

Figure 1.1   Immersed in ash at the base of Eyjafjallajökull, May 2010

highlights a moment where habitual tendencies and expectations are necessarily overturned in favour of haphazard interactions that prompt collective forms of action and re-orientation. The process of collecting together, assembling, and forming relationships through movement brings to the foreground our ability to move across boundaries and thresholds of identity, modes of thought, location, perception, and action. Movements that harness the relational and affective intensities of the situation—that unsettle, disrupt, or re-route our individual actions—offer new ways to collaboratively experience mobilities.

Focusing on Packing

The act of packing a bag is emblematic of a processual, everyday performance of mobilities that tourists undertake. It is a complex negotiation with a range of material and spatial qualities and movements, forging relationships between ourselves, the bag, the task at hand, and the situation we are within. It highlights the overlapping of everyday and mundane mobilities within larger global transitions and tourism ideals. Merging experiential, ethnographic, and theoretical perspectives, *Everyday Practices of Tourism*

Mobilities considers how relationships are formed during packing and travel and how these may attune us to collective and affective experiences. As a result of these attunements, questions arise regarding the boundaries of human and nonhuman action, and how our experiences reflect the flexibility, dissolution, and reconfigurations of these boundaries. Mobilities, when understood as the complex assemblages of individual movements and larger systems and the relations formed through movement, reveal how interconnected and co-dependent our movements are.

Packing is an activity that we have all experienced. Whether on a holiday with family, on a round-the-world backpacking trip, travelling for work, relocating or migrating, or simply packing a handbag or school bag for the daily commute, packing objects in and out of a bag is a practice that is experienced in a variety of different settings and for a range of purposes. This book focuses on how packing is a practice that unfolds in tourism situations, specifically within dormitory-style hostelling accommodation. Numerous people are in close proximity to each other, sleeping in bunk beds and sharing bathroom facilities. Bunk beds are strewn with towels, hand-washed clothes, and assorted personal items. Almost always you will find someone frantically sorting through their bag, as all of their belongings (including their underpants) are upturned and out on display for the dormitory occupants to see. Communal dormitory spaces present a hive of activity that offers a certain kind of atmosphere in which collaborative and social interactions often emerge (Murphy 2001; Oliveria-Brochado and Gameiro 2013), which makes it perfectly suited for studying practices of mobilities. Often the fleeting or heightened moments of intense interactions during packing become the everyday experience for tourists in hostels.

From this hothouse of intense and heightened activity, an experience emerges that begins to overcome human–nonhuman boundaries of interaction. Packing reveals interactions that deviate from habitual expectations of mobile proximities and spatial boundaries. By 'packing', I am not only referring to filling an empty bag; I am alluding to the small and often overlooked or under-considered moments when we directly engage with materials that we have brought with us and have around us. These may be our clothes, toiletries, the bags themselves, souvenirs, the surface of the floor we are packing on, or the space between the bunk beds where the bag is stored. The packing process encompasses a space that is beyond the perimeter of the bag, extending past the areas on the floor of the hostel room where the individual is packing (Figures 1.2 and 1.3). Objects move in and out of the bag, and we move in and out of rooms, around beds, and so on. As objects are located, collected, and moved into arrangements, they spill out on the floor, are strewn around the room, and then collated, reassembled, and moved back into the bag. Packing might be a procedural, organised,

Figure 1.2 Photograph of myself packing, situated amongst six people's belongings intermingled on the floor of a hostel dormitory room in Nepal

Figure 1.3 A tourist sitting on their backpack while trying to close the zip

and purposeful activity where we know in advance what we want to bring; or it can be the impulsive, 'running late', or hasty experience of travelling.

The practice of packing reveals an intersection of a number of concerns surrounding how mobilities encompass relational and collective processes. Reflecting on the packing process, one tourist stated, 'I'm packing and unpacking so often . . . It becomes part of your everyday . . . it becomes, going through the motions in a way'. As an ongoing daily interaction, packing reveals how we organise ourselves by sifting through objects, discarding or consuming items. It is a practice that draws attention to the various modes of relation between and across material and spatial qualities, in terms of navigating who and what we are travelling with, the social and lived experiences of spaces, or the co-construction and consumption of environmental and socio-cultural ideals of how and where we are moving. In this way, individual actions are never isolated but are always bound within collective processes. The practices that individuals generate to adapt and move with these collective concerns are indicative of the relationships that form and re-form through mobilities. Packing, as an everyday practice of tourism mobilities, contributes to the way we understand ourselves, our position in the world, and the ways in which we move.

Despite the fact that packing is an essential part of tourism—we pack before, during, and after each trip—there have been few studies that have examined packing and the myriad of experiences, sensations, movements, and practices that it encompasses. While the following studies investigate packing in various situations, there are limitations and differences to the approach that I deploy in this book. The materiality of the 'travel bag' is explored by Gavin Jack and Alison Phipps (2005) as an analogy for tourism experiences. The object of the bag becomes a metaphor for their fieldwork experiences while staying in various tourist accommodation sites on the Isle of Skye in Scotland. For Jack and Phipps, the bag is read as a 'text' (2005, p. 66), which can uncover stories, experiences, and interactions. Jennie Small and Candice Harris (2012) explored the gendered roles and differences in packing through interviews with academics travelling for conferences about the specific things (such as objects, clothing, or tools) that they brought with them. They found that the relationships between gender and identity was produced and reinforced through what was packed, which stabilised the gendered identities of the academic tourists. Similarly, Kenneth Hyde and Karin Olesen analysed media content and internet sources for advice on packing for air travel (2011) through video ethnography to explore how the items packed were used as props for 'constructing self-identity' (2012, p. 91). The notable study by Neil Walsh and Hazel Tucker (2009) examined how a backpack, as a material artefact, co-produces and performs the identity of 'backpacker' tourists (see further discussion in Chapter 2). Although there are only a scarce few studies, they all highlight the importance of packing in tourism experiences. Jack and Phipps point out that packing 'is the subject of stories' (2005, p. 50). Packing is a practice that everyone can relate to, and that everyone has experienced in one way or another.

In this book, I take an innovative approach by situating packing as an ongoing tourist practice that is interactive, performative, and generative. I document and survey this mundane, everyday routine to argue that packing is an example of an everyday practice of mobilities that involves negotiations of materiality, spatiality, and environmental ideals.[1] Packing is a situation where there is an increase in one's attunement to the way that we construct relationships as we move, and how these individual movements feed into larger collective concerns and practices. Of course, this process is embedded in a series of larger systems and processes that feed into, and are incorporated by, the practice of packing.

Packing can be a haphazard process that never seems to go according to plan (Figures 1.4 and 1.5). Another tourist that I interviewed explained:

> I just always put my [laughing] sleeping bag in the bottom, and then just, on top everything else. I try to have a system, but it's not always working [laughs] . . . It's a problem with the sleeping bag, it's in the bottom and then you take it out, you can open the bottom [of the bag], but then everything falls down and then, [laughing] yeah, you sort of have to unpack.

Moving one item means moving all the contents of the bag and often the bag itself, too. Movements are beyond the usual expected boundaries of singular objects—materials merge and become fluid as they interact with each other

Figure 1.4 A tourist packing on the roof of the hostel in Kathmandu, Nepal. Often ample room is required to spread out items during packing

Figure 1.5 A variety of packing practices

and with the person that is packing. Movements are never straightforward. It is a complex situation but also a common experience that that provides the perfect mix of constraint and complexity to track, analyse, and respond to mobile practices.

Focusing on packing a bag allows for an 'unpacking' of two key themes: collective interactions and global mobilities. Together, these two themes are informed by and intertwined within this book's inquiry into the everyday mobile practices of tourists and their encounters with materiality, spatiality, and environmental ideals. Through these themes, packing is examined as a situation where tourists become attentive to the way that their individual actions are entangled within larger global mobilities. I demonstrate that the practices developed during transit assist in honing our abilities to extract collective modes of knowledge from a variety of mobile situations and interactions.

Collective Interactions

Tourism situations offer many instances where actions are collective rather than individual, for instance when we participate in a tour group, walk down a busy city street, or sleep in a hostel dormitory. Often the focus in tourism is on human action and how we interact and share space with other tourists, when in fact there are a myriad of other nonhuman actors present and active in any given scenario (Haldrup and Larsen 2010; Urry and Larsen 2011). I am using the term *actor* as a broad outline of the many humans and nonhumans that give rise to actions, in line with actor-network theory usage. Bruno Latour states that '*any thing* that does modify a state of affairs by making a difference is an actor' (2007, p. 71, original emphasis; see also Lien and Law 2011; Van der Duim, Ren and Jóhannesson 2012). In this manner, a human, a tourist destination, an object, a weather front, a backpack, and so on can all be termed actors under this broad usage. There are a myriad of actors that support and enable our movements and that connect us to even more actors. Tourism situations are exemplary of how we navigate and collectively move with an array of nonhuman and human actors.

The collective situation in packing is played out across various scales and types of actors. Humans and nonhumans move together in momentary assemblages that collect through movement: from the luggage tags scanned by the baggage handlers at the airport, to the miniature 'travel-sized' toiletries, to the vaccines we get prior to departure, the passports and visas, or the ideals that motivate tourist flows. Collective actions, whether corporeal or imaginative actions, are enacted through momentary assemblages of humans and nonhumans, material and immaterial actors. Alongside the growing reconceptualisation of the role of matter and materiality in the social sciences, humanities, and arts (Barad 2003, 2007; Barrett and Bolt 2013; Bennett 2010; DeLanda 2006; Dolphijn and van der Tuin 2012; Latour 2007; Law 2004), practices of tourism mobilities foreground the intensity and agency that material actors hold in many mobile situations (Franklin 2003, 2014; Lund 2013; Michael 2000; Picken 2010; Walsh and Tucker 2009; Van der Duim 2007). As Rene Van der Duim states, 'tourism is held together by active sets of relations in which the human and the nonhuman continuously exchange properties' (2007, p. 964). The circulation of objects, ideas, cultures, and practices relies on vast mobilities networks and systems (Urry 2016) that move with us, aiding, restricting, or re-routing our intended movements. Each movement emerges from the interrelations of actors of various sizes, shapes, and capacities (Barad 2007). The bags we travel with and the objects we put in these bags are just one example of how we are always moving collectively.

In the past decade, the study of tourism has emphasised the knowledges that are generated by tourism and mobilities. Often the interactions that we have in-transit become 'a mode of knowing' (Carter 1987, p. 25), where tourist actions engage in multi-sensual experiences that respond to interactions, processes, and aesthetic resonances of new surroundings (Birkeland 1999; Crang 1999; Crouch 2004; Lean 2012; Sverrisdóttir 2011). Tourists are one of the many forms of nomadic subjects (Braidotti 2012) positioned in a constant state of transition that is always in contact with, and pushing the boundaries of, human and nonhuman action. To become 'nomadic', in this sense, is to push away from anthropocentrism and give rise to an array of possible interactions where human–nonhuman entanglements and moments of collective experiences can be felt and sensed. Because studies of tourism are frequently more object-oriented (Van der Duim 2007, p. 964), there is a risk that scholars treat nonhumans as 'resources' that are shifted 'around in other things such as suitcases, sneezes, bank accounts and keepsakes' without questioning the roles or capacities that they encompass (Picken 2010, p. 255). The problem lies in the fact that tourism *is* supported by a range of nonhuman materials which are resources (transport, electricity, fresh water, and so on) that are limited, costly, and often exploitative (Gren and Huijbens 2012; Urry 2016). Without regard to the nonhuman actors that are on the move with us, the danger is that tourism inevitably 'entails the exertion of force upon the earth, moulding its surface into marketable form' (Huijbens 2015, p. 200). Tourism, when considered solely within anthropocentric forces, runs the risk of isolating it from other forms of mobilities that contribute to the vast networks of actors that are moving. Therefore, this book takes up the imperative to examine how being always in the collective, that is, on the move with an array of actors, heightens and intensifies the situated aspects of our daily mobilities and informs the way our practices of movement can become transformative.

The actions occurring during packing are frequently communal and collaborative, reflecting the kinds of engagements with materials, spaces, and environments that can be considered to be generative of new experiences and modalities. In such moments we become aware of how we compose, combine, and reconfigure ourselves to fit within this constant state of flux and collective transition. It is a composition, a state where our movements merge actors into specific configurations of action. If you think of the process of 'composing oneself', when we pause and consider our actions before proceeding in a situation, it may seem as if you are not affected by the situation, but in fact, you are registering your relationships to (and perhaps differences from) the actions occurring. In this vein, 'composing' is the process of assemblage and of consistency (Deleuze and Guattari 2004, pp. 361–366), in which the term 'composition . . . underlines that things have been put together . . . while retaining their heterogeneity' (Latour 2010, pp. 473–474). This process of assemblage, of collecting together actors—human and nonhuman, material and immaterial—is precisely why packing is a perfect situation to examine the collective actions in tourism mobilities. During packing, and travel in general, decisions are not necessarily based on conscious knowledge or rehearsed procedures. Rather, they are often indicative of how tourism initiates a series of situated, experiential, and sensory engagements from which we extract creative tendencies and apply the innovations they foster to daily life and ongoing interactivity. The actions occurring during packing reflect the vast array of conditions that are collecting in that particular moment. Packing is just one example of movements where we interact with a variety of nonhuman and human actors through performative and collaborative processes. The result is a messy yet mundane engagement with the surrounding situations through which new mobilities arise.

Globalised Mobilities

With the increasing movement of people around the globe, we encounter complex alignments of human and nonhuman actors that develop into collective experiences. Over one billion international journeys are undertaken annually, and with a current growth rate of four per cent (UNWTO 2016), people travel for reasons spanning leisure, work, migration, and refuge. There is urgency that we reconsider the impact and scale of our movements. Ideals of a nomadic (Western) lifestyle sit in contrast to the rising threat of global ecological crisis that the Anthropocene era propels (Gren and Huijbens 2014, 2016; Palsson et al. 2013). With the increasing scale of international movements, tourism needs to be considered as a 'geophysical force that is part of the relationship between humanity and the Earth' (Gren and Huijbens 2014, p. 7). The fact that international tourist mobilities are enabled by a range of actors (Haldrup and Larsen 2010; Van der Duim, et al. 2012; Walsh and Tucker 2009; Urry 2011, 2016) necessitates a collective and relational understanding of our movements. It is the practices required of each mobile person and the intersection with a range of social, cultural, and environmental complexities that compels attention.

It is important to acknowledge that this inquiry is focused on tourists staying in hostelling accommodation. I want to stress, however, that people are in-transit for a range of reasons, not necessarily just for leisure, which the term 'tourist' implies (Currie, Campbell-Trant and Seaton 2011; Week 2012). The tourists that I have interviewed do not all fit within the 'backpacker' archetype either (see Hannam and Ateljevic 2007; Sørensen 2003). While the majority of tourists that I interviewed did use backpacks (see Chapter 2), their motivations for travelling, the things they had brought with them, and their stories that they shared did not fit into the simplistic identity of a 'youthful backpacker' staying in a hostel. Tourists are just one of the many mobile subjects (Braidotti 2012; Lury 1997; Urry and Larsen 2011) but it is crucial to recognise the privilege and ability possessed by the majority of tourists. Although many people do not have the luxury or ability to undertake international travel, it is the processes and experiences of transiting that I draw on as applicable to both tourism scenarios and everyday mobilities. I presume most of the tourists I encounter, including myself, have the 'right' passport, able bodies, and enough wealth to provide access to safe transit. It is important to note that hostelling also provides low-budget accommodation and people stay in hostels for a range of reasons. The point is that people are travelling and nomadic for a range of different reasons and motivations. Whether travelling for leisure, work, or other reasons, tourists are well positioned to notice the multiplicities of transitions, collective, and relational formations through their interactions.

Studying mobilities encompasses a search for understanding the variety of ways our movements are constantly shifting from the macro to the micro, or from the globalised to the everyday. As a field of research and a practice of movement, the term mobilities highlights the way our movements and actions are mobilised and interrelated with an array of actors (Adey, Bissel, Hannam, Merriman and Sheller 2014; Elliott and Urry 2010; Urry 2011). The many ways that humans and nonhumans move and interact can be 'seen as a set of highly meaningful social practices that make up social, cultural and political life' (Adey et al. 2014, p. 3) and produces new, creative, and experiential modes of orienting ourselves as both individuals and collectives. John Urry's significant contribution to the field pinpoints the extent and variety of mobility experiences, which are 'moving assemblages of humans, objects, technologies and scripts' (2011, p. 26) that are infused in an assortment of corporeal, imaginative, objective, virtual, and communicative movement practices (pp. 24–25). Mobilities are an assemblage of interactions and sensations. It is also imperative that we pay attention to the techniques of attuning to movement. Registering the sensation of movement encapsulates the process of being 'a sensing body in movement . . . that is always tending, attending to the world' (Manning 2013, p. 2). My interest lies in expanding upon the conception and execution of movement, especially where there is potential to affect more than the individual (human) forms that initiate, or are implicated in, the movement. Therefore, this focus on packing helps in understanding the relationships formed through macro and micro, individual and collective movements.

When the boundaries of our movement are entwined with other actors, when we can feel the relations forming as we move, align, and attune to the affective resonances of the situation, it is precisely these moments when our individual intentions are reconfiguring in favour of collective mobilities. How we apply these experiences of mobility to a variety of situations and across a range of scales signals the complexity of techniques that are required as we oscillate from local and global connections, and through individual and collective practices.

Site-Specificity: Iceland and Nepal

There is often a slight disjunction between environmental experiences that immerse us and the mundane daily negotiations that we have while travelling. Certain destinations may intensify or evoke different kinds of experiential or situated attunements to our processes of moving and transiting. From the outset of this research, I have wondered if a destination with unique environmental features—such as tumultuous weather patterns or iconic geological sites—would increase our attention to, and perception of, the material or spatial qualities in daily activities after we had experienced immersive, environmental qualities. For example, after gazing at an erupting volcano, would our attention to the subtler, daily tasks of packing a bag, washing clothes, or walking to the convenience store need to adjust? Would the immense scale and saturation from these 'environmental' encounters alter the perception of our everyday actions? There is not always a clear boundary around how the environment shapes our experiences, and vice versa. We must change as our surroundings change. The conditions that are seemingly extraneous, which are encountered when arriving at a destination, require the consideration of an entirely new set of factors. To this end, the term 'environment' needs to be reconceptualised. An environment is a set of conditions (such as the terrain, climate, human and nonhuman inhabitants) that coordinate and produce experiences through interactions with actors moving with-and-in that specific composition. How tourists reorient to these conditions and align their ideals with such experiences can take on drastically unexpected and exciting actions if they are open to registering these influences.

To address the influence that the environment of a destination has on tourists' practices, this book focuses on tourist experiences in Iceland and Nepal. These two countries are idealised tourist destinations that conjure many expectations and desires. Preconceived notions of a destination fit within a cultural imaginary comprising social, environmental, and spatio-geographical influences to be consumed and experienced. Tourists often approach a destination with these ideals overlaid onto what actions they expect to undertake. But once on the ground, the environmental conditions, such as changes in seasons or weather, differences in culture, or bodily adjustments after transit, can and do overwhelm tourists (Anderson 2015; Sverrisdóttir 2011). It is this point of transition, when we become aware of how our movements respond to the specific destination we are within, that prompts tourists to move with these conditions in order to orient themselves. These are moments of affective resonances in which collective forms of movements are brought to the forefront of our sensory registers.

Destinations such as Iceland and Nepal encompass many sites that excite a socio-cultural and geographical imaginary. They are sites where tourists are thrown into situations with complex environmental influences. In the imaginations of many tourists, Nepal is the gateway to the Himalayas, often described as verging on the *top of the world* (Figure 1.6). Similarly, Iceland is often described as being on the *edge of the world*, since it touches the Arctic Circle and is marketed by its spectacular geological sites (Figure 1.7). The overlap of these imaginaries is strategically exploited by marketing campaigns that impose on both destinations ideas of uniqueness and naturalness, and of experiential forms of tourism (Benediktsson, Lund and Huijbens 2011; Frohlick 2003; Lund 2013; Oslund 2005).[2] Tourists are influenced by the idealised conceptions of each environment as a unique and experiential tourist destination.

Preconceived and imaginary notions of a destination contrast with actual experiences when on-the-ground. This is where the disjuncture or disconnect between immersive, environmental experiences contrasts to the more mundane or everyday practices that tourists undertake. It is the point at which ideals confront or conflict with experiences and sensations that provides an opening for examining how our idealised mobilities intersect with collective experiences.

Figure 1.6 The Annapurna Himalayan range, visible from above the city of Pokhara, Nepal

Figure 1.7　Snæfellsjökull, the iconic 'entry point' to the centre of the earth in Jules Verne's novel, visible from the Icelandic capital city, Reykjavík

How to Pack a Bag: a Reader's Guide

The two themes of this book—the collective interactions and globalised mobilities—encapsulate the multitude of practices and theories that respond to the complex movements and relationships that the practice of packing a bag presents and that this book attempts to track. The result is a cohesion of many methods into specific actions that rely upon new disciplinary approaches to present the many ways we study and practice being in-transit and experiencing mobilities. This merger and meshing of theoretical ideas and practical experiences ultimately defines the practical, critical, abstract, and relational sensitivities we employ each day in-situ.

Even at this early stage, it is important to acknowledge the blurring of my own experiences as both researcher and tourist, as the lure of the unfamiliar and exotic landscapes I was surrounded by saturated my research processes. Caroline Scarles describes the feeling of being a 'researcher-as-tourist', in which the researcher's intentions are blurred with the 'anticipation' of the touristic experiences that are the subject of study (2010, p. 914). My 'practices' as a tourist were inseparable to my situated practices as a researcher. I was open to the haphazard and often unexpected moments that unsettled my expectations for what kind of data I would collect, or the intensity and affective resonances of the situations I found myself within. I embraced an ethnographic approach that 'does not need to "capture" or "arrest" the flow of everyday life, but to follow it, and to gain a *sense* of it' (Pink 2012, p. 33, original emphasis). By 'practicing' packing, by living out of a backpack for months on end, and by becoming a mobile, nomadic subject, sleeping in dormitory rooms and hanging out in communal hostel spaces, the way that I was *doing* research (Law and Singleton 2013, p. 485) harnessed these practices and sensations of the entangled nature of mobile ethnographic research.

The photographs and interviews throughout this book were conducted during two fieldwork trips to Iceland and Nepal, where I stayed for almost six months in hostels.[3] I interviewed fellow guests in the hostel about how they packed their bags and took time-lapse photographs of them as they packed their bags. I also documented my own packing throughout the fieldwork. Almost 24,000 photographs were taken,[4] documenting forty-nine participants, plus my own daily packing-rearranging-unpacking-repacking routines. Most of the photographs are of people packing bags, but some were of touristic, idealised framings of the destination, or my experiences of each place.

The photographs serve not merely to re-present experiences, but to offer alternative perspectives into the packing process. They capture individual and collective experiences that traverse sites and situations, feelings, sensations, and affects. Working against representation or as concrete evidence of a moment, the photographs are indicative of the many subtle, fleeting, and momentary entanglements of collective actions. Most of the photographs of people packing were taken in time-lapse sequences (a series of photographs taken several seconds apart, like a stop-motion video), and were taken with a longer exposure (1/8 second), so that the movements of people's bodies, the materials being packed, and the bag itself would be traced. The result is a lingering movement of actors in negotiation, rendered visible in the photographic traces (Figure 1.8). They 'unlock the

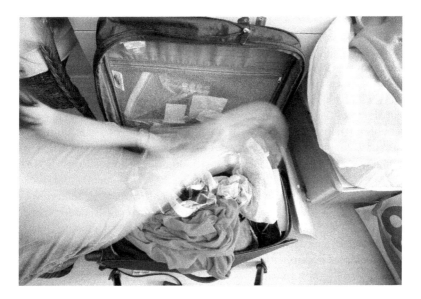

Figure 1.8 Blurred traces of packing movements captured in a photograph

expression of encounters', which are moments that are often challenging to express in language alone (Scarles 2010, p. 918). In this manner, the photographs are non-representational, seeking to 'rupture, unsettle, animate, and reverberate rather than report and represent' (Vannini 2015, p. 19), while attending to the relational movements and affective intensities of the situation (Thrift 2007).

In addition, my background as an artist and practice-led researcher informs and shapes the research and practice deployed in this book. Using a mixture of visual ethnographic methods, practice-based exploration, and creative outputs (see Barry 2016), I traverse 'packing' as a *practice* that is creative, generative, collaborative, and experiential. In creative arts there is a long history of practice-led research which values material interactions and in-situ experiences that necessarily blur the researcher-practitioner relationships (Bolt 2004; Barrett and Bolt 2013; Carter 2004; Chilton and Leavy 2014; Witzgall, Vogl and Kesselring 2013). Creative approaches are attentive to the complexity of 'practical knowledges, the materials of practice and the novel situation' (Bolt 2004, p. 6). Practice-led research foregrounds the relational modes of production that move across the disciplinary trends of accumulating knowledge, in order to emphasise embodied and situated knowledge acquisition.

The result is a postdisciplinary study which congeals practical and theoretical influences, using them as required for the specific line of inquiry. Postdisciplinary research is a reflexive approach that follows themes of inquiry through a range of techniques. In tourism and mobilities studies, postdisciplinarity is increasingly acknowledged as necessary to tracing and tracking mobile subjects (Coles, Hall and Duval 2009; Hollinshead and Ivanova 2013; Gill 2012; Urry 2016, p. 6). Calls for 'new transdisciplinary research spaces' (Adey et al. 2014, p. 3) echo the practice-led approach in which mobilities research needs to be considered 'as a force that animates fields, creating connections as it moves, while growing and benefiting from that diversity' (p. 4). John Urry suggests that 'thinking through a mobilities "lens" provides a distinctive social science that is productive of different theories, methods, questions and solutions' (2016, p. 18) and is ultimately postdisciplinary (p. 6). Consequently, the book shifts back and forth between practical examples from the interviews, photographs, fieldwork experiences, and the theoretical notions and concepts surrounding movement, mobilities, and spatial practices. The assemblage of approaches that I have gathered and deployed is a reminder of the complex multiplicities of actors that are interconnected by increasingly globalised movements.

This book traces the intricacies and relations emerging through packing, and the connections to an array of actors entwined in tourism situations and everyday experiences of movement. In Chapter 2, the practice of packing is connected to the material interactions of tourists and the formation of mobile experiences. An examination of materiality, as the interactions between human and nonhuman actors, leads to new collaborative situations emerging. Chapter 3 focuses on how these material conditions also require negotiating spatial boundaries and perceptions. The hostel dormitory is examined as a situation that primes tourists to move collectively rather than individually when negotiating communal spaces. In Chapter 4, I discuss how the environment of the destination is firstly idealised by tourists, but then, upon arrival, can conflict or force tourists to adjust to unexpected or immersive conditions. Two case studies in Iceland and Nepal highlight the disjuncture and then realignment of tourists' experiences, where the sensations of the moment blur with the mundane or everyday activity of packing. It is in these moments where tourists begin to sense and feel the entanglement with the environment, resulting in collective experiences of movement. Finally, in Chapter 5, I discuss how the actions undertaken during packing create awareness of the possibilities and movements beyond ourselves and our own individualised actions and motivations. The acknowledgement of the collective processes in tourism positions movements to be increasingly open to affective and collaborative forms of mobility.

The book traverses the practices and theories that the activity of packing a bag brings to the foreground. The resulting contribution emphasises the importance of how packing, and other everyday tourist practices, are embedded within complex mobilities that cross individual and collective experiences, and local and global tourist imaginaries and cultures. These practices connect our seemingly mundane or routine tasks to global flows of tourism and mobility, and in doing so, reveal the relevance and potentiality for alternative, collaborative tourist experiences and everyday practices of mobilities.

Notes

1 I am using the term 'ideals' with two interrelated meanings. In the first instance, touristic 'ideals' refers to how ideas and expectations of tourism are performed and constructed. Tourism relies heavily on the imagination and desires of people travelling and experiencing certain kinds of situations, landscapes, and cultures. These are often image-based expectations that occur through the marketing and branding of destinations that are shared via promotional materials, guidebooks, and social media (Bærenholdt, Haldrup, Larsen and Urry 2004; Haldrup and Larsen 2010). Secondly, I am referring to the aesthetic and multi-sensory registers that contribute to our imaginations of certain places. Tourists often draw from past experiences or shared stories and recommendations that circulate in tourist cultures. In this manner, touristic ideals manifest in the expectations and imaginations that tourists use to mediate, perform, and evaluate their experiences.

2 Both Iceland and Nepal have a relatively young history of tourism. In Iceland, during the 1950s there were just over 4,000 tourists each year (Icelandic Tourist Board 2016), yet in recent years, tourism is rising by over 20 per cent annually, to just over 1 million tourists entering the country (UNWTO 2016). Nepal has only been accessible for internationals since the 1950s (Ministry of Culture, Tourism and Civil Aviation 2013), and in 2014 almost 800,000 tourists entered (UNWTO 2016). It is important to note that tourism in Nepal has been drastically impacted by the 2015 earthquake which devastated the country, seeing tourism drop in 2015 to approximately 550,000 international entries (UNWTO 2016).

3 The fieldwork trips were conducted in May–July 2012 and September–December 2013. Forty-nine participants were recruited who were guests at hostels in Reykjavík, Iceland (at *Reykjavík Downtown* and *Reykjavík Loft*) and Kathmandu, Nepal (at *Alobar1000 Hostel*), and a small pilot study in Berlin, Germany (at *Circus Hostel*).

4 An excerpt of a video compilation of the photographs can be seen at: www.youtube.com/watch?v=5TDdeWFtntg

References

Adey, P., Bissel, D., Hannam, K., Merriman, P. and Sheller, M. 2014. 'Introduction'. *In*: P. Adey, D. Bissel, K. Hannam, P. Merriman, and M. Sheller, eds. *The Routledge handbook of mobilities*. New York: Routledge, pp. 1–20.

Anderson, J. 2015. 'Exploring the consequences of mobility: Reclaiming jet lag as the state of travel disorientation', *Mobilities*, vol. 10, no. 1, pp. 1–16. doi:10.108 0/17450101.2013.806392

Bærenholdt, J.O., Haldrup, M., Larsen, J. and Urry, J. 2004. *Performing tourist places*. Aldershot and Burlington: Ashgate.

Barad, K. 2003. 'Posthumanist performativity: Toward an understanding of how matter comes to matter', *Signs*, vol. 28, no. 3, pp. 801–831.

Barad, K. 2007. *Meeting the universe half way: Quantum physics and the entanglement of matter and meaning*. Durham and London: Duke University Press.

Barrett, E. and Bolt, B. eds. 2013. *Carnal knowledge: Towards a 'New Materialism' through the arts*. London and New York: I.B. Tauris.

Barry, K. 2016. 'Diagramming: A creative methodology for tourist studies', *Tourist Studies*. First published online before print: Nov 28, 2016. doi:10.1177/146879 7616680852

Benediktsson, K., Lund, K.A. and Huijbens, E. 2011. 'Inspired by eruptions? Eyjafjallajökull and Icelandic tourism', *Mobilities*, vol. 6, no. 1, pp. 77–84. doi:10.1080/ 17450101.2011.532654

Bennett, J. 2010. *Vibrant matter: A political ecology of things*. Durham: Duke University Press.

Birkeland, I. 1999. 'The mytho-poetic in northern travel'. *In*: D. Crouch, ed. *Leisure/tourism geographies: Practices and geographical knowledge*. London: Routledge, pp. 17–33.

Birtchnell, T. and Büscher, M. 2011. 'Stranded: An eruption of disruption', *Mobilities*, vol. 6, no. 1, pp. 1–9. doi:10.1080/17450101.2011.532648

Bolt, B. 2004. *Art beyond representation: The performative power of the image.* London and New York: I.B. Taurus.

Braidotti, R. 2012. *Nomadic theory: The portable Rosi Braidotti.* New York: Columbia University Press.

Carter, P. 1987. *The road to Botany Bay: An essay in spatial history.* London: Faber and Faber Ltd.

Carter, P. 2004. *Material thinking: The theory and practice of creative research.* Carlton: Melbourne University Press.

Chilton, G. and Leavy, P. 2014. 'Arts-based research practice: Merging social research and the creative arts'. *In*: P. Leavy, ed. *The Oxford handbook of qualitative research.* Oxford: Oxford University Press, pp. 403–423.

Coles, T., Hall, M.C. and Duval, D.T. 2009. 'Post-disciplinary tourism'. *In*: J. Tribe, ed. *Philosophical issues in tourism.* Bristol: Channel View Publications, pp. 80–100.

Crang, M. 1999. 'Knowing, tourism and practices of vision'. *In*: D. Crouch, ed. *Leisure/tourism geographies: Practices and geographical knowledge.* London and New York: Routledge, pp. 238–256.

Crouch, D. 2004. 'Tourist practice and performances'. *In*: A. Lew, C. Hall and A. Williams, eds. *A companion to tourism.* Malden, MA: Blackwell, pp. 85–95.

Currie, R.R., Campbell-Trant, T. and Seaton, S. 2011. 'Joining the in-crowd: Symbols for backpacker identity', *International Journal of Culture, Tourism and Hospitality Research*, vol. 5, no. 1, pp. 47–56. doi:10.1108/17506181111111753

DeLanda, M. 2006. *A new philosophy of society: Assemblage theory and social complexity.* London and New York: Continuum.

Deleuze, G. and Guattari, F. 2004. *A thousand plateaus: Capitalism and schizophrenia*, trans. B. Massumi. London: Continuum.

Dolphijn, R. and Van der Tuin, I. eds. 2012. *New materialism: Interviews and cartographies.* Ann Arbor: Open Humanities Press.

Elliott, A. and Urry, J. 2010. *Mobile lives.* London and New York: Routledge.

Franklin, A. 2003. *Tourism: An introduction.* London: Sage.

Franklin, A. 2014. 'On why we dig the beach: Tracing the subjects and objects of the bucket and spade for a relational materialist theory of the beach', *Tourist Studies*, vol. 14, no. 3, pp. 261–285. doi:10.177/1468797614536331.

Frohlick, S.E. 2003. 'Negotiating the "global" within the global playscapes of Mount Everest', *Canadian Review of Sociology and Anthropology*, vol. 40, no. 5, pp. 525–542.

Gill, A. 2012. 'Travelling down the road to postdisciplinary? Reflections of a tourism geographer', *The Canadian Geographer/Le Géographe canadien*, vol. 56, no. 1, pp. 3–17. doi:10.1111/j.1541-0064.2011.00400.x

Gren, M. and Huijbens, E.H. 2012. 'Tourism theory and the earth', *Annals of Tourism Research*, vol. 39, no. 1, pp. 155–170. doi:10.1016/j.annals.2011.05.009

Gren, M. and Huijbens, E.H. 2014. 'Tourism and the anthropocene', *Scandinavian Journal of Hospitality and Tourism*, vol. 14, no. 1, pp. 6–22. doi:10.1080/15022 250.2014.886100

Gren, M. and Huijbens, E.H. eds. 2016. *Tourism and the Anthropocene.* London: Routledge.

Haldrup, M. and Larsen, J. 2010. *Tourism, performance, and the everyday: Consuming the orient*. Oxon and New York: Routledge.

Hannam, K. and Ateljevic, I. 2007. 'Introduction: Conceptualising and profiling backpacker tourism'. *In: Backpacker tourism: Concepts and profiles*. Clevedon: Channel View Publications, pp. 1–8.

Hollinshead, K. and Ivanova, M. 2013. 'The multilogical imagination: tourism studies and the imperative for postdisciplinary knowing'. *In*: M. Smith and G. Richards, eds. *Routledge handbook of cultural tourism*. Routledge: Abingdon, Oxon and New York, pp. 53–62.

Huijbens, E.H. 2015. 'Topological encounters: Marketing landscapes for tourists'. *In*: G.T. Jóhannesson, C. Ren, and R. Van der Duim, eds. *Tourism encounters and controversies: Ontological politics of tourism development*. Farnham: Ashgate, pp. 201–220.

Hyde, K.F. and Olesen, K. 2011. 'Packing for touristic performances', *Annals of Tourism Research*, vol. 38, no. 3, pp. 900–919.

Hyde, K.F. and Olesen, K. 2012. 'Assessing the grounded theory of packing for air travel using a video-ethnographic case study'. *In*: K.F. Hyde, C. Ryan and A.G. Woodside, eds. *Field guide to case study research in tourism, hospitality and leisure*. Bingley, UK: Emerald, pp. 89–107.

Icelandic Tourist Board. 2016. *Foreign visitors to Iceland 1949–2015*. Reykjavik: Icelandic Tourist Board/Ferðamálastofa. Retrieved 22 March 2017 from: www. ferdamalastofa.is/static/files/ferdamalastofa/Frettamyndir/2016/april/foreign-visitors-to-iceland-1949-2015.xls

Jack, G. and Phipps, A. 2005. *Tourism and intercultural exchange: Why tourism matters*. Clevedon, Buffalo and Toronto: Channel View Publications.

Latour, B. 2007. *Reassembling the social*. New York: Oxford University Press.

Latour, B. 2010. 'An attempt at a "compositionist manifesto"', *New Literary History*, vol. 41, no. 3, pp. 471–490.

Law, J. 2004. *Matter-ing: Or how might STS contribute?* Lancaster: Centre for Science Studies, Lancaster University. Retrieved 20 July 2016 from: www.lancaster. ac.uk/fass/resources/sociology-online-papers/ . . . /law-matter-ing.pdf

Law, J. and Singleton, V. 2013. 'ANT and politics: Working in and on the world', *Qualitative Sociology*, vol. 36, no. 4, pp. 485–502. doi:10.1007/s11133-013-9263-7

Lean, G. 2012. 'Transformative travel: A mobilities perspective', *Tourist Studies*, vol. 12, no. 2, pp. 151–172. doi:10.1177/1468797612454624.

Lien, M.E. and Law, J. 2011. '"Emergent Aliens": On salmon, nature, and their enactment', *Ethnos: Journal of Anthropology*, vol. 76, no. 1, pp. 65–87. doi:10.1 080/00141844.2010.549946

Lund, K.A. 2013. 'Experiencing nature in nature-based tourism', *Tourist Studies*, vol. 13, no. 2, pp. 156–171. doi:10.1177/1468797613490373

Lury, C. 1997. 'The objects of travel'. *In*: C. Rojek and U. John, eds. *Touring cultures: Transformations of travel and theory*. London and New York: Routledge, pp. 75–95.

Manning, E. 2013. *Always more than one*. Durham, NC: Duke University Press.

Michael, M. 2000. 'These boots are made for walking . . .: Mundane technology, the body and human-environment relations', *Body and Society*, vol. 6, no. 3–4, pp. 107–126.

Ministry of Culture, Tourism and Civil Aviation. 2013. *Nepal tourist statistics 2012*. Kathmandu: Government of Nepal, Ministry of Culture, Tourism and Civil Aviation; Policy, Planning and Infrastructure Development Division: Documentation, Research and Statistics Section. Retrieved 15 January 2017 from: www.tourism. gov.np/uploaded/TourrismStat2012.pdf

Murphy, L. 2001. 'Exploring social interactions of backpackers', *Annals of Tourism Research*, vol. 28, no. 1, pp. 50–67.

Oliveira-Brochado, A. and Gameiro, C. 2013. 'Toward a better understanding of backpackers' motivations', *Tékhne*, vol. 11, pp. 92–99. doi:10.1016/j.tekhne.2013. 11.001

Oslund, K. 2005. '"The North begins inside": Imagining Iceland as wilderness and homeland', *GHI Bulletin*, vol. 36, Spring, pp. 91–99.

Palsson, G., Szerszynski, B., Sörlin, S., Marks, J., Avril, B., Crumley, C., Hackmann, H., Holm, P., Ingram, J., Kirman, A., Buendía, M.P. and Weekhuizen, R. 2013. 'Reconceptualizing the "Anthropos" in the Anthropocene: Integrating the social sciences and humanities in global environmental change research', *Environmental Science and Policy*, vol. 28, pp. 3–13. doi:10.1016/j.envsci.2012.11.004

Picken, F. 2010. 'Tourism, design and controversy: Calling on non-humans to explain ourselves', *Tourist Studies*, vol. 10, no. 3, pp. 245–263. doi:10.1177/ 1468797611407757

Pink, S. 2012. *Situating everyday life: Practices and places*. London: Sage.

Scarles, C. 2010. 'Where words fail, visual ignite: Opportunities for visual autho-ethnography in tourism research', *Annals of Tourism Research*, vol. 37, no. 4, pp. 905–926. doi:10.1016/j.annals.2010.02.001

Small, J. and Harris, C. 2012. 'Packing through the ages: Gender and age related behaviour around packing for conference travel'. *In: CAUTHE 2012: The new golden age of tourism and hospitality, Book 2*. Proceedings of the 22nd Annual Conference. Melbourne: La Trobe University, pp. 567–571.

Sørensen, A. 2003. 'Backpacker ethnography', *Annals of Tourism Research*, vol. 30, no. 4, pp. 847–867. doi:10.1016/S0160-7383(03)00063-X

Sverrisdóttir, H. 2011. 'The destination within', *Journal of the Association of Icelandic Geographers/Landabréfið*, vol. 25, pp. 77–84.

Thrift, N. 2007. *Non-representational theory: Space, politics, affect*. London: Routledge.

UNWTO. 2016. *Tourism highlights, 2016 edition*. Retrieved 3 February 2017, from: www.e-unwto.org/doi/pdf/10.18111/9789284418145

Urry, J. 2011. 'Does mobility have a future?' *In*: M. Grieco and J. Urry, eds. *Mobilities: new perspectives on transport and society*. Farnham: Ashgate, pp. 3–20.

Urry, J. 2016. *Mobilities*. Cambridge: Polity Press.

Urry, J. and Larsen, J. 2011. *The tourist gaze 3.0*. London: SAGE Publication Ltd.

Van der Duim, R. 2007. 'Tourismscapes: An actor-network perspective', *Annals of Tourism Research*, vol. 34, no. 4, pp. 961–976. doi:10.1016/j.annals.2007.05.008

Van der Duim, R., Ren, C. and Jóhannesson, G.T. eds. 2012. *Actor-network theory and tourism: Ordering, materiality and multiplicity*. Oxon: Routledge.

Vannini, P. ed. 2015. 'Non-representational research methodologies: An introduction'. *In*: *Non-representational methodologies: Re-envisioning research*. New York and Oxon: Routledge, pp. 1–18.

Walsh, N. and Tucker, H. 2009. 'Tourism "things": The travelling performance of the backpack', *Tourist Studies*, vol. 9, no. 3, pp. 223–239. doi:10.1177/1468797610382706

Week, L. 2012. 'I am not a tourist: Aims and implications of "travelling"', *Tourist Studies*, vol. 12, no. 2, pp. 186–203. doi:10.1177/1468797612454627

Witzgall, S., Vogl, G. and Kesselring, S. eds. 2013. *New mobilities regimes in art and social sciences.* Farnham: Ashgate.

2 Everyday Material Practices of Tourists

Tourists experience a range of encounters with materials in everyday tasks and procedures. Examining the materiality of everyday experiences reveals the interconnected and immersive character of our seemingly singular movements. Every action highlights the production and composition of alternative modes of interaction with an array of actors. Packing a bag provides a specific instance to analyse the material conditions, performative aspects, and interactions that arise in mobile situations.

In this chapter, I explore how materially driven experiences unfold in tourism scenarios and become part of everyday routines while travelling. I suggest that material practices are necessarily developed by tourists in everyday actions, and that these are used to generate alternative forms of experiences that are collaborative and enriching. Materiality, in this vein, has two key functions as a process and a concept, which transgresses its discursive origins. It points to an inclusive and affirmative understanding that all actors—whether material or immaterial, human or nonhuman—are integral to the physical, cultural and experiential registers of a situation.

An anecdote of a scene that I witnessed in a hostel provides a good starting point and will suggest the scope and complexity of examining practices that are driven through material interactions. I had just checked in to a hostel in Reykjavík, Iceland, located my ten-bed mixed dormitory room, and I opened the door to find two people sitting on a large suitcase, while another person was shoving items of clothing in through the open seam on the side. 'His airport shuttle leaves in twenty minutes', one of the guys who was half kneeling, half sitting on top of the suitcase said to me, as if this could explain why he was perched precariously on top of somebody else's overflowing suitcase. 'I couldn't find my passport so I had to unpack everything', explained the owner of the suitcase, as he paused to wave his passport in hand triumphantly. The three of them were frantically stuffing things in the side of the suitcase, which looked like it had exploded. Glancing down, I realised that I was standing on some of his clothes that had spilled out on the floor. 'Here, let me help you', I said, handing them the clothes. Finally, the suitcase closed, the zipper firmly shut. Passport in hand, he ran out, thanking us. In this instance, four previously unacquainted persons became bound together in action. The emphasis of material processes, of achieving the 'packed bag' as end goal, highlights a moment in tourism where procedural tendencies and expectations (such as notions of personal space and social etiquette) are necessarily overturned in favour of haptic, collaborative, and material interactions. Packing is a specific example of the material conditions and interactions that are engaged during travel, but also in regular everyday routines.

Re-thinking materiality allows us to examine how we move alongside a mass of materials, transgressing the traditional boundaries of human and nonhuman action. Collective forms of movements arise where action is no longer tied to individualised subjective decisions. The growing emphasis on materiality in many disciplines is useful to demonstrate instances in tourism that harness experiences of materials while in-transit or on the move in daily life. This is made evident through the daily material procedures that tourists undertake which are indicative of such mergers of practical 'hands on' engagements and conceptually driven ideals and expectations of tourism experiences. These actions blur the polarities of being stationary 'at home', or mobile and travelling 'away', thus creating a greater awareness of practices that merge the everyday with the touristic.

It is important to begin the discussion by emphasising the need to reconceptualise the role of material relations and what they indicate for our ability to negate the global culture of tourism and mobilities. Materiality draws attention to the intersection of global tourism cultures with the often unnoticed everyday practices that are developed. In this chapter, I outline examples of tourist practices, that is, ways that materials are encountered during packing, focusing on how material interactions provide conditions from which communal and collaborative experiences can arise. I show how material assemblages are instigated through the process of packing a bag (whether it is a suitcase, backpack, or other luggage), which feeds into the representation of tourist cultures, particularly the backpacker, but also present complex and entangled forms of movement. Next, I draw from my own experiences, interviews, and photographic documentation with fellow tourists staying in hostels to 'unpack' the material encounters that foster collaborations between humans and nonhumans. Finally, when considered together, these theories, practices, and examples demonstrate that materiality allows us to think and practice alongside a range of human and nonhuman movements.

Mobile Material Practices

There is an increasing prevalence to recognise, encompass, and expand on how experiential knowledges are generated through material encounters. Although there is strong emphasis on the importance of the interrelations that increasing mobilities bring to a global society (Adey, Bissel, Hannam, Merriman and Sheller 2014; Elliot and Urry 2010; Sheller and Urry 2004; Urry 2011), there is room to expand on the role of materiality and the relational aspects of mobilities. Considering tourism as a set of mobile material practices requires close scrutiny of how experiences are produced and the strategies that are developed while on the move. To this end, investigating the role of materials and the resulting materially driven interactions occurring in tourism situations provides ways to better understand this increasing global mobility and provide alternative and nomadic forms of practice. Understanding daily interactions with materials in tourism that move beyond traditional notions of individualised subjectivity reveals how these expanded processes can afford collaborative engagements.

The daily practices that tourists undertake indicate an assortment of material interactions. In the most obvious instance, materially driven practices are tactile encounters where human bodies and material substances come into proximity and contact with each other. Processes that open awareness to aesthetic and relational qualities of materials—the sensual, embodied, or processual interactions—provide foundations for the decisions, motivations, and actions that are undertaken by both individual tourists and within broader mobile cultures. A materially driven practice in tourism might be experienced in obvious tourist activities, such as walking around the destination, going on organised tours, or visiting themed attractions, museums, galleries, or bars. However, the more mundane or routine daily tasks of cooking, washing, conversing, sleeping, packing a bag, sorting through personal items, and so on, are also materially driven practices. These various material encounters motivate further experiences across a range of actors. The manner in which tourists and researchers understand these material interactions is important to consider in terms of how they contribute to everyday experiences. Not all moments in tourism are glamourous, breathtaking, or leisurely. Knowledge and experience can arise in a variety of activities; some are expected and anticipated, and some are subtle, mundane, or fleeting to such an extent that they can be easily overlooked.

The agency that nonhuman material actors hold in mobile situations compels further inquiry into how and why practices that are inherently material are carried out. There is growing emphasis on the importance of materiality in travel and the role materials play in the formation of tourist experiences

(Currie, Campbell-Trant and Seaton 2011; Franklin 2014; Haldrup and Larsen 2010; Urry and Larsen 2011; Van der Duim 2007; Van der Duim, Ren and Jóhannesson 2012). Although there have been many notable studies that present 'tourism as a knowing practice' (Crouch 2004, p. 90; see also Crang 1999; Haldrup and Larsen 2010; Lean 2012; Sheller and Urry 2004; Urry 2003, 2011; Urry and Larsen 2011), the question of *how* these practices are carried out and the materials that aid these practices can be teased out further.

Attention to the nonhumans that we travel with—the materials in our bags and the composition of our surroundings—implies that individual actions are always in relation to a collective. Obviously, this is not usually at the forefront of tourists' intentions or actions, and tourist movements are often motivated purely for an individualised access and consumption of an experience. There are many claims that the field of tourism studies has overlooked the potential role that nonhuman actors play in tourism (Franklin 2003, 2014; Lund 2013; Palsson 2013; Picken 2010; Walsh and Tucker 2009; Van der Duim 2007). Felicity Picken explains that the study of tourism needs to acknowledge that nonhuman actors are 'essential to the human constructed world' (2010, p. 248) and therefore need to 'include material relations' (p. 246) as integral to the touristic experience. It is the 'thingness' of tourism (Franklin 2003, p. 103) that co-constitutes the experiences, sensations, and stories that tourists acquire. Therefore, vastly different conceptualisations and methods are needed to move past the human/nonhuman and subject/object dualisms in order to evaluate the extent that material actors contribute to touristic experiences.

Finding new ways to study the multi-sensual, embodied, and affective encounters in tourism can trace previously indiscernible relationships and affordances that form as we move with and through the world (Barry 2016; Franklin 2014; Jensen, Gyimothy and Jensen 2015; Jensen 2009). Across tourism and mobilities, scholars are calling to embrace new methodological approaches that shed light on the alternative forms of knowledge and experiences of our movements (Adey et al. 2014; Büscher and Cruickshank 2009; Coles, Hall and Duval 2009; Hollinshead 2010; Hollinshead and Ivanova 2013; Merriman 2014). Habits, routines, and mundane, ordinary practices (Edensor 2007; Hui 2012) are infused in tourism experiences. Moments of pausing, reflecting, waiting, queuing, long-haul transiting, and so on (Anderson 2015; Bissell 2007; Bissell and Fuller 2011) might 'demand a considerable amount of time, attention and practiced negotiation' (Barry 2016, p. 1). These more mundane mobilities that tourists encounter every day, which are so ordinary, subtle, or even fleeting, are a starting point to examine the materially driven practices that tourists partake in. These mundane, banal, and invisible moments, although quite unremarkable at the time, offer entirely different vantage points on action and situations. Although they are often in contrast to the spectacular or heightened touristic actions, materially driven practices give rise to new experiences, creative knowledges, and collaborative situations. Materials form part of the heterogeneous qualities of the ways in which tourists navigate through and establish relationships.

Understanding the experiences and knowledges formed through material interactions aligns with actor-network theory inspired analysis, where actions undertaken assist in harnessing the potential of multiplicities in every encounter (Beard, Scarles and Tribe 2016; Latour 2007, 2014; Law and Singleton 2013; Lien and Law 2011; Mol and Law 1994, 2007; Van der Duim 2007; Van der Duim, Ren and Jóhannesson 2012). These oscillatory movements of experience, from localised production in an individual's subjective actions to a broader conception of global multiplicities, provide a relational framework in which, as Bruno Latour notes, *the collective* emerges (2007, p. 172). Latour's proposition of collective action, focused through materially driven interactions, allows us to understand how connections are formed and how such encounters produce new connections (Latour 1996, p. 231).

During transit, encounters with materials are often social, sometimes playful (Sheller and Urry 2004; Thrift 2007), and usually strenuous. As we explore and negotiate daily tasks, we generate 'activity with immense affective significance' (Thrift 2007, p. 7). These performances are often materially driven, as '[t]ourists are always dependent on non-humans . . . and their material agencies' (Gren and Huijbens 2012, p. 162). They are movements that are enacted through the vast network of actors, both human and nonhuman. Because we learn by doing, and repeating doing becomes a practice (Marchland 2010, p. 7), we are enacting processes and new relationships with/in the world (Mol 2002, pp. 32–33). As Trevor Marchland posits, 'becoming knowledgeable is not a matter of assembling information . . . but rather knowledge is formed in everyday activities and knowing is conterminous with our movement *through* the world' (2010, p. 5, original emphasis). Materially driven practices are an integral part of 'knowledge-growing' (Ingold 2010, p. 116) that aid our understanding of where and how we situate ourselves in relation to the world.[1] This involves tracing and examining the 'relationships between actors in practice' (Beard et al. 2016, p. 78) to hone in on how these practices form new networks and experiences. Knowing through experience reveals the mechanisms (O'Sullivan 2006, p. 44) that allow orientation and adjustment to our everyday movements and interactions.

Each transition and destination presents an array of new relations that require a repositioning of the tourist's actions and the priorities to enact the required processes. The example of packing a bag highlights a range of interrelated processes, for instance in a search for an item within the bag at an airport check-in counter, or trying to sort dirty from clean clothes in a dormitory room. Relations emerge through a 'convoluted network with a multiplicity of highly diverse dates, places and people' (Latour 1996, p. 231). These emergent actions compose propositions for material encounters through interaction between actors.

To return to my earlier example of the three people packing one suitcase, there are personal, social, and material boundaries that are being redefined through such actions. Questions of personal space, of interaction and social cues, as well as the inherent materiality of the actions, compel further scrutiny of this 'hands on' collaboration. A new materialist understanding of these practices is an assertion that all actors (human and nonhuman) are 'composed of—or are reducible to—matter, material forces or physical processes' (Stack in Bolt 2013, p. 2). Alongside the increased attention given to 'matter' in the social sciences (Barad 2008; Latour 2007; Law 2004), recent discussions on materialism across the arts, humanities, and social science disciplines have emerged within the discourse on 'new materialism' (Alaimo 2010; Barrett and Bolt 2013; Bennett 2010; Braidotti 2012, 2013; DeLanda 2006; Dolphijn and van der Tuin 2012; Grosz 2005, 2008, 2011). It builds on the foundations in ANT and Science and Technologies Studies (STS) that all actors have agency that is distributed through interactions (Barad 2003, 2007; Law 2002, 2004; Law and Hassard 1999; Latour 1990, 1996, 2007, 2014). Examining a situation through a new materialist lens emphasises that the material composition of actors, such as the body packing, the suitcase, or the events that constitute tourism processes, may be regarded as a vital element in each action.

Overcoming the dualisms of human/nonhuman and the subject/object distinction has been a prevailing goal in the new materialist approach. Heavily influenced by Gilles Deleuze and Félix Guattari's advocacy for 'affirmative difference' (2004), and propounded by Rosi Braidotti's notion of 'nomadic theory' (2006, 2008, 2012), materiality is positioned as a set of relationships that operate across actors (Deleuze and Guattari 2004). The points at which we 'cease to be subjects to become events' (Deleuze and Guattari 2004, p. 262) are where individual subjectivities and conscious decisions and actions are collectively bound. Braidotti's affirmation of the body as material is bound through fluid, reflexive movements with the environment (2008, p. 183). The importance of considering our bodies through materiality is echoed by many theorists, such as Jane Bennett's prompt to think of ourselves as entwined in ecologies and assemblages of materials (2010). Shifting the emphasis from concepts to processes, Braidotti suggests that nomadic thinking could be used to 'identify possible sites and strategies'

(2012, p. 14) where materiality—released from a classical definition of materiality or individualised anthropocentric experience—is crucial to be a subject-in-formation. Process, affect, and inter-action 'cannot be reduced to human, rational consciousness' (Braidotti 2012, p. 2). As Jane Bennett explains, '[m]ateriality is a rubric that tends to horizontalize the relation' by drawing our attention 'toward a greater appreciation of the complex entanglements of humans and nonhumans' (2010, p. 112). Materiality points to an even more inclusive understanding of 'material' in which the physical descriptions of matter, the cultural value of materials, and the experiences of relationships formed through material interactions (within and beyond the human) are all components.

The opening example of communal packing gives prominence to a destabilising of socio-cultural expectations through material interactions. Obviously not all packing experiences are as communal as my example here. But in hostel dormitories, the shared social space is conducive of a communal atmosphere where collaborative situations happen unexpectedly. These 'disruptions' to our habits, routines, and expectations may be unsettling (Veijola, Molz, Pyyhtinen, Höckert and Grit 2014, p. 4), but can provide the conditions for new ways of being with that are collective and transformative. For instance, the physical boundaries between guests in a hostel dormitory are slim, so there is a little more 'openness' to individual actions being on display, and invitation for people to pitch in and lend a hand, as my example demonstrated. Even when packing a bag in isolation, such as in the comfort of your own home, the material interactions lend themselves to a practical and hands-on approach in which your body and the materials being packed come into direct contact. It is these moments of negotiation, movement, and displacement of bodies and objects through the process that an inquiry into the material practices encompassed in packing is merited.

Unpacking the Collective

Material practices point to a specific kind of interaction that is focused on material qualities and processes instead of a more general or universal notion of substance. The shift from the analysis of individual movements to the consideration of collective assemblages of materials 'retunes attention towards to the assemblages of matter that move' (Adey et al. 2014, p. 267). Latour noted the urgency for taking materiality as a 'concern' (2007, pp. 87–120) in which every actor—every *thing*—holds potential to influence and inter-act with every other thing (Latour 1990, 2007). Tourism is an assemblage of actors who momentarily coalesce into networks (Beard et al. 2016; Van der Duim, Ren and Jóhannesson 2012). These networks might be formed through specific actions or processes (such as packing, going on a tour, or an international flight), or they might be part of the broader global mobility networks that govern how, where, and why we are moving.

The selections and decisions that tourists make about the materiality of their bags and the items that they travel with are integral to the overall experience they have. Lightweight luggage, miniature 'travel sized' toiletries, and a well-read guidebook might enhance or smoothen our transit experiences. Or, chaos can easily unfold when packing becomes a momentous task, when the zip on the bag breaks, or the support straps on a hiking backpack no longer hold. These unexpected material actions make the ability to traverse the hostel or hotels, taxi ranks, cobbled streets, check-in counters, and many other places that tourists travel with their bags difficult or even impossible (see Walsh and Tucker 2009). Often the material compositions that we move with are critical in determining how action unfolds. Packing a bag presents an opportunity to consider both the micro textures of our movements and the macro mobilities that are enacted. I interviewed and observed people with a range of bag styles and sizes. I asked about the type of bag they used to try to evaluate whether the style, shape, or capacity of the bag influenced their packing techniques. However, I observed that regardless of the style of bag, the process still required negotiating materials in complex ways, whether using a hiking backpack, a travel backpack, or a suitcase.

Backpacks are generally anywhere from 40–90 litres in capacity, whereas a 'daypack' is a small supplemental backpack of only 15–40 litres. There are several types of backpacks. A 'hiking' backpack is designed so that the main entry is through the top of the bag. Hiking backpacks are generally taller and thinner, aimed at keeping the bag adjacent to the back while it is worn. The 'travel' style backpack generally has an opening and access to the interior compartment via a zipper, thus allowing it to open similar to a suitcase. Travel backpacks are usually easily lockable, converting into a sort of duffle-bag when fully closed, while some even include wheels at the base that are able to be folded away or covered up (Figure 2.1).[2] Suitcases range in size from aircraft cabin-size carry-on bags of only a few dozen litres to large suitcases with the capacity of far more than a backpack (90+ litres) (Figure 2.2). Of course there are many other styles, sizes, and designs of bags, depending on the purpose, duration of travel, and personal preferences. However, these three main 'categories' that I have briefly outlined here are indicative of how bags fit within broader sets of material, technological, and socio-cultural considerations that negate how and where we travel. The material considerations of selecting a bag for travel highlight the complexity of inter-related actions that tourists foresee their movements bound within. For instance, the hiking backpacks are often constructed with canvas or Gore-Tex materials that protect them from longer exposure

Figure 2.1 Packing a hiking bag

Figure 2.2 Packing a carry-on sized suitcase

periods of precipitation while out hiking, whereas a suitcase with wheels that pivot 360° make for 'effortless' manoeuvring through bustling airport check-in areas. And the cabin-sized carry on suitcases are moulded to stack uniformly on their side in the overhead lockers in aircrafts. The selection of bag and the marketing, construction, and usage contributes to the broader 'transit aesthetics' (Barry 2015) of mobile tourist cultures that material interactions are embedded within.

Thirty out of the forty-nine tourists I interviewed used backpacks, whereas sixteen used suitcases, and three used carry-on sized bags or other means (such as bike panniers) as their main travel bag. In Iceland, I met two tourists who used tiny little daypacks as their sole bag. One was on a short trip of only several days; and the other tourist had purposefully brought very little so that she could swap, discard, and acquire clothes and necessities as she travelled. There was one tourist I met in Nepal who was on a cycling trip through Asia, so their 'bag' was comprised of four bicycle panniers. Running throughout these observations about tourists' choices of bags and the materials that they bring within the bags is the overarching sense that materials tourists travel with are selected and negotiated in very personal ways. It also dispels the myth that the tourists staying in hostels are all 'backpackers', a tourist archetype that defines the individual based on the materiality of their backpack.

There are countless works that describe and define backpacking tourism as a subcultural category of tourists who travel for leisure, on a budget, and are generally younger and focused on having social experiences (Cohen 1973; Murphy 2001; Pearce 1990; Richards and Wilson 2004; Uriely, Yonay and Simchai 2002). It is not my intention to give a historical overview of the rise, theorisation, or practice of backpacking as a tourist phenomenon. However, many argue that the backpacker identity is far from a homogenous group (Cohen 2011; Hannam and Ateljevic 2007; Sørensen 2003), although they do fit into the ideal of the 'global nomad' (Richards and Wilson 2004) and might frequently distance themselves from being classified as 'tourists' (Week 2012). What emerges from the majority of research is that the backpack—as a material object—is often isolated to the production of an identity that is humanistic, inherently individual, and locked within the construction of the social realm of the backpacker identity. However, it is important to note that the bag itself—commonly a hiking backpack, positioned high upon one's back—defines how backpacker tourists are seen as 'cultural symbols' (Richards and Wilson 2004, p. 3). This visible 'performance of a specific tourist identity' (Walsh and Tucker 2009, p. 224) is what sets the social practices of 'backpackers' apart from other tourists. It is the backpack, as a material artefact, which brings 'social realities into being' (Walsh and Tucker 2009, p. 225) and merges the tourist body with tourism cultures (Picard 2012, p. 2) through the materiality of an object. Due to the fact that the tourists I interviewed use a variety of different kinds of bags, and many were not self-identifying themselves explicitly as 'travellers' or 'backpackers' (Week 2012), the cultural identity of a backpacker tourist can only take the examination of material practices so far.

There is one notable study by Neil Walsh and Hazel Tucker (2009) that is quite close to my approach of examining interactions between tourist's bodies and their bags. Walsh and Tucker present the many ways in which a backpack, as a material artefact, co-produces the identity of 'backpacker' tourists. Their argument closely resembles my exploration: to examine how materials—specifically the backpack—contribute to and induce intensified experiences of travel. Importantly, they recognise that '[b]ackpacking is *supported* by a huge assembly of specific objects (2009, p. 224, original emphasis), and it is these subtleties that I also draw on to propel this book's inquiry. For example, they fuse the backpack with the body, recounting how a heavy backpack rubs against the shoulders of the body carrying it. Using examples from their own backpacking experiences, Walsh and Tucker open up the possibility that in some instances material *things* act with a resonance and vitality, rather than just as passive intermediaries. While the object of the backpack does indeed become an actor, there are limits in how backpacking, as a subculture and identity, can explore the interactions that occur between tourists, their bags, and the connections to everyday mobility practices. As Nigel Thrift observes, the linking of processes to the object 'cannot be reduced to it' (2007, p. 111) and needs to be considered, like all actors, as 'an ongoing rearrangement of objects and symbols within a field involving the body' (p. 116). Although the bag itself is a material object that does *act*, it is important not to present the backpacker subculture at the foreground of how and why tourists act alongside their bags as they move.

Packing is a negotiation of tourist cultures, material technologies, and personal habits and preferences. This means that the process of packing is an ever-evolving performance as tourists balance between their individual ideals and collective influences. Viewing the packing process as performative brings forth the 'ability to alter the ways in which we perceive things in the world' through materialised interactions, transforming our practices to attend to 'affective perceptual experiences' (Colman 2007, p. 72). While increased awareness of the distributed agency across humans and nonhumans helps place our individual actions within global mobilities, it is these micro moments, these fleeting material encounters, that have 'the ability to make things happen, to produce effects' that must be investigated (Bennett 2010, p. 5). Thinking of packing and everyday tourist practices in this way helps to understand how experiences that challenge our presumptions can have such an affective power. In this vein, materiality connects and forges new relationships across actors, generating relations that can be beyond ourselves and beyond our own subjective individual decisions.

Moving With Materials

Simply locating one item within the bag presents a mammoth task of dismantling carefully placed items and decanting these onto the floor, the bed, or into spare hands. The body of the person packing flits in and around opening and closing elements. The zipper pulls tightly, catching the fabric. One item leaks and suddenly the clothes and the floor are covered in a soapy residue. This frenzy of complex movements occurs between the person packing, the items in the bag, the material of the bag itself, the surfaces of the architecture they are within, and the spatio-temporal shifts occurring in that particular place. These moments challenge our presumptions of our ability to interact and collaborate with a realm of actors. Although fleeting, such encounters begin to open up a realm of modes of understanding and thinking through our everyday movements, and through multiplicities of both local and global scales.

By observing packing and practicing it myself, what became clear was the transformation of objects away from singular forms towards a collective mass of material that is being negotiated (Figure 2.3). Of the forty-nine

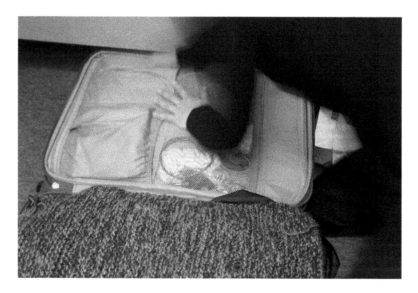

Figure 2.3 The body of a tourist leans over the bag, pressing down on the bag in preparation to close

tourists I spoke with and photographed, thirty-six said they had a specific strategy for packing. They said they had an order or approach that they used every time they packed, or a routine of how to arrange items within their bags. Six tourists said they had a specifically 'rolled' their clothing items, while twenty-one said they layered or folded things before placing them in the bag. Most evident was the strategy of collating objects with an intensified consideration of the material properties such as the size, texture, density, weight, and so on. Comments were made such as, 'I try to keep it in order . . . my socks first, then my pants, and then . . . my T-shirts'. Another said they grouped clothing together, explaining that,

> Underwear [goes] together in one bag . . . and then T-shirts in one, and pants and sweatshirts in another . . . so that way it's all like, if I want to change my underwear or something I know where it is . . . I keep them together.

Others said they grouped according to size and weight, 'shoes in the bottom, and big stuff in the bottom', one tourist explained. Many people that I observed and photographed grouped in accordance to specific material qualities or uses. For example, they would gather soft things around fragile items, shoes with socks, or rain and outdoor wear together in water-tight packets. A common approach was manipulating the materials to compress and combine things together. 'I like to roll things up and it makes things a lot smaller', one person remarked. Tourists frequently mentioned a range of strategies they had learned and acquired from a range of sources, such as websites and online forums, guidebooks, or advice from their friends and family or fellow tourists. One person noted that they took inspiration from the infamous product design and packaging of IKEA, explaining that everything in their suitcase is laid 'flat across the bottom . . . like building blocks . . . that's what they do at IKEA—flat packing'. Many tourists commented on the fact that there seemed to be a 'right' and a 'wrong' way to pack, or some kind of intuitive process that you are meant to have when packing. Several tourists, myself included, reflected on how they do a 'test pack' before going on a longer trip. One person described the process of 'test packing' was to 'figure out how much I could fit in my backpack, because I knew I wanted to carry very little'. There is much speculation and discussions between tourists in hostels about how to be a 'good' packer or a 'fast' packer, as if it is something that can be inherited or learnt that will somehow improve the quality of our travels.[3]

The variations of descriptions and types of measurements used, for example the weight, texture, substance, or categories, disclose the many different roles that materials take on in this process. Depending on the movements required, materials are regarded in different ways, making the material elements oscillate between singular forms and a fluid material array of sensitive and responsive actors. What began to emerge from these interviews is that in the rigorous daily process of packing, objects transform away from individual entities into fluid, malleable substances: a mass of material that is being negotiated.

The words that tourists frequently used to describe the process are also indicative—terms such as 'squish', 'squeezing', or 'stuffing', indicating how each object was being transformed into a fluid mass of material in the process. This transformation of objects from singular to multiple aligns with John Law's acknowledgement that 'the singularity of an object is precarious, uncertain and revisable' (2002, p. 36). Or, as I am proposing, this mode of experiencing materials through processual encounters reveals materiality in a fluid form, unfixed from specific representations and forms. Elizabeth Grosz (2005) also describes how in certain circumstances, materials have the ability to shift between objective, solid representational forms and malleable, fluid matter. Emerging 'out of and as substance', *things* (material entities) have the ability, through their transgressive potential, to open our awareness to alternative modes of experience and sensation (Grosz 2005, p. 133). These subtle material negotiations have the potential to create situations in which materials are intensified to the degree that they have the potential to overcome their own material forms and constraints. Considering 'matter as activity' (Alaimo and Heckman 2008, p. 245) presents a way to reconceptualise materiality as not being fixed or static. Under certain conditions, these nomadic, processual movements and encounters could be something that is, to borrow Grosz's term, 'beyond the material' (2011, p. 17), where matter is 'not a thing but a doing, a congealing of agency' (Barad 2008, p. 173). In other words, when relationships emerge that are beyond ourselves (as singular materially comprised entities), an increased awareness and sensing of communal movements occurs. This, of course, can only happen through material processes that connect into other potential sets of relations. Necessarily overturning singular identities in favour of collective actions signals a shift in habitual processes and the formation of material practices and knowledges.

While packing, movements that blur the boundaries between the usual usages and arrangement of objects and bodies highlight how materiality can become nomadic, fluid, and relational. As one person recounted, 'to get all my stuff in my bag I was like rolling on it and sitting on it and kicking it, trying to get everything to squish in'. Although subtle, similar examples are frequent in packing, inducing alternative ways that tourists move with their material belongings. The materials are constantly being re-negotiated and assessed as to whether they are useful, necessary, fragile, prone to leakage, and so on. The roles of each material object and the expectations of the person packing are constantly being negotiated as they move into proximity through the rigorous interactions. In addition to demonstrating the material practices that tourists partake in, packing allows us to consider the materially driven and collective experiences that bring together emergent and often unanticipated experiences.

In the packing process, movements occur that increase our sense of something that is greater than ourselves and greater than the objects that are being packed. The intensive act of packing, where materials and bodies move together, allows a consideration of a 'nonunitary vision of the subject' (Braidotti 2012, p. 3) as the boundaries of each material entity are momentarily blurred. Agency is no longer isolated to a singular or human subject, offering compositions of material agency that are entangled across actors. The boundaries between the body and the bag are set into flux. It is in the flexing of materiality that we are made aware of the *more-than* (Manning 2009) potential of forces larger than ourselves. Erin Manning calls the movement between materials and bodies 'the not-yet that composes the more-than-one' (2009, p. 13). This is appropriate because movements are in the moment, but are not quite actualised; they are influenced by existing structure yet do not determine where an action will come to rest or what the effects are going to be. In these moments, the notions of identity, individuality, and subjectivity are set askew and put into motion, ready to be opened up, explored, and examined.

Manning goes on to describe how the affective movement of subjectivity is 'across bodies, across resonances of life, some of them human, many of them non-human. Affect is what returns, not the subject' (2010, p. 126). For the tourists I interviewed, as well as in my own personal experiences, these moments are hard to pinpoint and difficult to articulate, as often you feel immersed in this frenzied experience. As Latour reminds us, '[a]ction is not done under the full control of consciousness' (2007, p. 44). The focus shifts from simply itemising the objects within the bag, or selectively and consciously making movements, and it is at this point where the potential for greater sensory awareness and experiences emerges.

It is this more-than potential which provides an increased sense of something greater than ourselves emerging through the objects that are being packed. These moments within packing bring forth a consideration of the potential to experience relationships beyond ourselves as individuals. The newly formed relationships breach individuality and present collective interactions that, if only momentarily, fuse the experience of the human with the nonhuman. It is a moment that we experience relationally, inviting us to '[t]hink the object not ontologically but processually' (Manning 2013, p. 32). A collective emerges that leads to further participation and movement across experiences of actors. The result is a situation that presents the ability to rethink the subject as a 'collective entity' (Braidotti 2008, p. 182). It creates movements through presumptions about individuals, desires, and actions, linked through the intensified practices that are part of the everyday routine of tourists.

As part of the interview process I took photographs documenting tourists unpacking and re-packing their bags. The photographs indicate this *collective action* unfolding, depicting a series of movements where material boundaries are reconfiguring as the bodies move with the bags. The photographs were taken as a time-lapse series with a longer exposure (1/8 second) to highlight the movements of the body, objects, and bag. My original intention of using photographic time-lapse was to track the position of each object as people packed. However, what quickly emerged after taking the first few series of people packing was the vibrant aesthetic that the photographs capture when the movements of people and objects appear blurred and streak across the image (Figure 2.4).

The photographs capture movement through a different spatio-temporal register. Movement and interaction can be seen as the blurring and hazed traces. Sometimes they fill the image, other times they are smaller and harder to identify (Barry 2017). These blurring, lingering moments begin to indicate

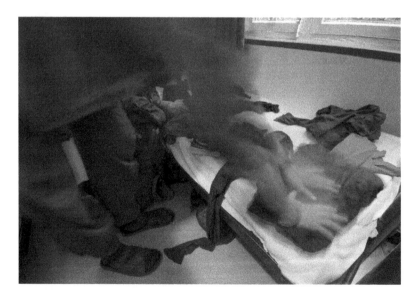

Figure 2.4 The hands rest momentarily on the clothes, attempting to hold the pile of materials in place. Seconds after this photograph was taken, the clothes sprang back and toppled all over the bed and floor

the instances where the many subtle negotiations of the person packing and the materials re-acting to their movements. The boundaries of movement are stretched and warped, ultimately resulting in a congealing of the material of the body and the bag. These movements of the collaboration between the body and the bag are observable, especially when an object is placed inside the bag and the hand and object move together in action. When the object is placed inside the bag, the bag often shifts slightly, moving in response, and setting the material boundaries into flux. The often frenzied attempts to unpack, sort, find, or re-pack reveal moments in which the materials—of the body, the bag, the objects—are moving in a manner greater than themselves, no longer singular entities but a collaborative collective action that flows with and in between the act unfolding (Figures 2.5, 2.6, and 2.7).

Within this process of packing material practices emerge that reveal movements that are greater than the individual, where materiality needs to be considered as more-than (Manning 2009) a property of a singular entity. In these materially driven practices attention must be given to the vast array of nonhuman actors and how they contribute to a collective action that is constantly unfolding in everyday procedures during travel. The many kinds of material practices in tourism, including but not isolated to the example of the packing process, present opportunities for how we situate ourselves using embodied, collaborative, and processual methods. In the instance of packing, this may arise through the manipulation of material qualities, as

Figure 2.5 Arms hovering above the bag as objects are moved in and out of the bag

Figure 2.6 Kneeling and pressing on the contents of the bag

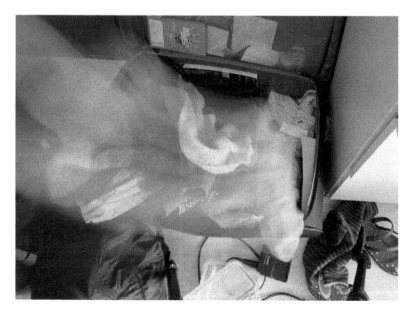

Figure 2.7 The blurred areas in the photograph capture the frenzy of material movements

we squish, squeeze, hold, press, or push. Or it can arise, as I outlined in the opening recollection, in assisting others in their packing. The simple act of sitting or kneeling on a bag suggests an array of interactions that induce collaborative and collective movements.

From Materiality to Spatial Encounters

The material interactions that tourists have during packing raise awareness of the movements and experiences that are beyond our individual actions. The experiences that tourists have during everyday, mundane, or routine activities may reveal experiences that are communal and collaborative in unexpected ways, and that can be used to generate collective forms of knowledge and experience. The practices that emerge offer a glimpse into intensified intersections of bodily and material experiences that encompass an array of actors—both human and nonhuman. Studies of tourism mobilities need to take on a fluid and reflexive approach that can adapt, mould, or merge experiences as we encounter each unique scenario. Much like the material entities that are transformed into fluid, malleable substances in the packing process, the approaches used to consider tourist practices can take into consideration a ream of material actors and events and may provide a basis for new forms of materially driven experiences.

The materials that humans are entangled with in any situation give rise to bodily sensations and registers. Therefore, it is important to consider tourist bodies as bound to and re-active to a range of materials. Understanding materiality in this way creates the potential to consider that, regardless of the material (or immaterial) composition, we are bound to all actors in a situation. Moments when individual subjectivities, decisions, and actions are drawn into the collective co-composition of movement (Deleuze and Guattari 2004) draws attention to the human and nonhuman entanglements that are in motion. The boundaries of ourselves (as individuals) are momentarily overturned in favour of collaborative experiences by rethinking what constitutes materiality.

Attentiveness to the process of assemblage allows uncertainties and tentative relations to surface (Law and Singleton 2013, p. 491). Studying how the collective emerges needs 'to attend to the multiplicity of formations without generalizing in advance about their agency or constitution' (Anderson, Kearnes, McFarlane and Swanton 2012, p. 213). In this way, the collective is inherently beyond the material, to echo Grosz (2011). While the term assemblage can refer to an action, it is also a new set of forms that emerges from newly connected networks (Anderson et al. 2012, p. 213). The ability to unpack and examine the many interrelations and actors that occur during packing insists on attentiveness to materiality and the complexity of relations that materials produce. These considerations of how collective actions produce sensations that can be felt across material and immaterial actors (Bolt 2013, p. 3) pave the way for the dissolving of human and non-human boundaries. The impulse to rethink what constitutes 'material' and 'matter' across disciplines indicates the importance of providing a more precise and situated set of relationships.

Examining the practice of packing through the concept of materiality reveals how collective experiences develop. This chapter began by reconceptualising materiality and highlighting the need for an increased awareness of material processes and the vibrancy of materials, which has become prominent in tourism mobilities. The study of mobile tourist practices needs to engage a range of approaches and propositions, seeing each investigation as a 'holistic endeavour' (Büscher and Cruickshank 2009, p. 2), which points to the need for an increased sensing and acting for communal and collaborative experiences. It is the practices in which materially driven interactions emerge that allow materiality to be understood as more-than the property of a singular entity (Manning 2009, 2013) to include a vast array of material nonhuman actors. Focusing on the movement, the event, and the experience of the co-constructed space helps determine how an array of actors contributes to a collective action that moves with material practices and spatial encounters. Developing the transformative potential of materiality necessitates an examination of our proximities to materials. This requires an examination of the spatial distribution of actors that are mobilised to tease out the way that relational movements are collective as we shift and forge relationships in various mobile encounters.

Notes

1 Creative arts literature has a long and established engagement with materially based practices and their capacity to enact transversal experiences and knowledges. See Estelle Barrett and Barbara Bolt's examination of knowing through creative and material practices (2007); Bolt's introduction of 'new materialism' and art practice (2013); Paul Carter's influential proposition of 'material thinking' (2004); Rosi Braidotti's discussions of transversal practices that allow us to think 'critically and creatively' (2013, p. 12) beyond individual or anthropocentric boundaries; and my analysis of transversality and material practices in tourism (Barry 2017).

2 For examples of different types of 'bags', see the categories for sale on the websites of the luggage company BlackWolf, sporting 'travel & trek', 'luggage', or 'daypacks': www.blackwolf.com.au/category/Packs/1; or North Face's selection of 'backpacks', 'technical packs', or 'luggage and duffels': www.thenorthface.com/shop/equipment

3 The introduction to Lonely Planet's latest book, which is dedicated just to packing tips, hints at the complexity and culture surrounding packing: 'An art, a science,

a necessary evil: packing is a task all travellers must tackle before their journey even begins. Not many of us, however, do it well, and even fewer of us approach it with any sense of pleasure' (2016, p. 4).

References

Adey, P. and Anderson, B. 2011. 'Anticipation, materiality, event: The Icelandic ash cloud disruption and the security of mobility', *Mobilities*, vol. 6, no. 1, pp. 11–20. doi:10.1080/17450101.2011.532919

Adey, P., Bissel, D., Hannam, K., Merriman, P. and Sheller, M. eds. 2014. *The Routledge handbook of mobilities*. New York: Routledge.

Alaimo, S. 2010. *Bodily natures*. Bloomington: Indiana University Press.

Alaimo, S. and Heckman, S. 2008. 'Introduction: Emerging models of materiality in feminist theory'. *In*: S. Alaimo and S. Heckman, eds. *Material feminisms*. Bloomington and Indianapolis: Indiana University Press, pp. 1–22.

Anderson, J. 2015. 'Exploring the consequences of mobility: Reclaiming jet lag as the state of travel disorientation', *Mobilities*, vol. 10, no. 1, pp. 1–16. doi:10.1080/17450101.2013.806392

Anderson, B., Kearnes, M., McFarlane, C. and Swanton, D. 2012. 'Materialism and the politics of assemblage', *Dialogues in Human Geography*, vol. 2, no. 2, pp. 212–215. doi:10.1177/2043820612449298

Barad, K. 2003. 'Posthumanist performativity: Toward an understanding of how matter comes to matter', *Signs*, vol. 28, no. 3, pp. 801–831.

Barad, K. 2007. *Meeting the universe half way: Quantum physics and the entanglement of matter and meaning*. Durham and London: Duke University Press.

Barad, K. 2008. 'Living in a posthumanist material world: Lessons from Schrödinger's cat'. *In*: A. Smelik and N. Lykke, eds. *Bits of life: Feminism at the intersections of media, bioscience, and technology*. Seattle: University of Washington Press, pp. 165–176.

Barrett, E. and Bolt, B. 2007. *Practice as research: Approaches to creative arts enquiry*. London: I.B. Tauris.

Barrett, E. and Bolt, B. eds. 2013. *Carnal knowledge: Towards a 'New Materialism' through the arts*. London and New York: I.B. Tauris.

Barry, K. 2015. 'The aesthetics of aircraft safety cards: Spatial negotiations and affective mobilities in diagrammatic instructions', *Mobilities*, first published online before print: Nov 2, 2015. doi:10.1080/17450101.2015.1086101

Barry, K. 2016. 'Diagramming: A creative methodology for tourist studies', *Tourist Studies*. First published online before print: Nov 28, 2016. doi:10.1177/1468797616680852

Barry, K. 2017. 'Transversal travels: The relational movements and environmental intensities of packing a bag', *Studies in Material Thinking*, vol. 16, pp. 1–17.

Beard, L., Scarles, C., and Tribe, J. 2016. 'Mess and method: Using ANT in tourism research', *Annals of Tourism Research*, vol. 60, September, pp. 97–110. doi:10.1016/j.annals.2016.06.005

Bennett, J. 2010. *Vibrant matter: A political ecology of things*. Durham: Duke University Press.

Bissell, D. 2007. 'Animating suspension: Waiting for mobilities', *Mobilities*, vol. 2, no. 2, pp. 277–289. doi:10.1080/17450100701381581

Bissell, D. and Fuller, G. eds. 2011. *Stillness in a mobile world*. Oxon and New York: Routledge.

BlackWolf. 2016. *BlackWolf: Packs*. Retrieved 2 November 2016, from: www.blackwolf.com.au/category/Packs/1

Bolt, B. 2013. 'Introduction: Toward a "New Materialism" for the arts'. *In*: E. Barrett and B. Bolt, eds. *Carnal knowledge: Towards a 'New Materialism' through the arts*. London and New York: I.B. Tauris, pp. 1–14.

Braidotti, R. 2006. *Transpositions*. Cambridge: Polity Press.

Braidotti, R. 2008. 'The politics of life as Bios/Zoe'. *In*: A. Smelik and N. Lykke, eds. *Bits of life: Feminism at the intersections of media, bioscience, and technology*. Seattle: University of Washington Press, pp. 177–192.

Braidotti, R. 2012. *Nomadic theory: The portable Rosi Braidotti*. New York: Columbia University Press.

Braidotti, R. 2013. *The posthuman*. Cambridge and Malden, MA: Polity Press.

Büscher, M. and Cruickshank, L. 2009. 'Designing cultures? Post-disciplinary practices'. *In*: *Proceedings of the 8th European Academy of Design Conference: Connexity*. Aberdeen: The Robert Gordon University.

Carter, P. 2004. *Material thinking: The theory and practice of creative research*. Carlton, VIC: Melbourne University Press.

Cohen, E. 1973. 'Nomads from affluence: Notes on the phenomenon of drifter tourism', *International Journal of Comparative Sociology*, vol. 14, pp. 89–103.

Cohen, E. 2004. 'Backpacking: Diversity and change'. *In*: G. Richards and J. Wilson, eds. *The global nomad: Backpacker travel in theory and practice*. Bristol, UK: Channel View Publications, pp. 43–59.

Cohen, S.A. 2011. 'Lifestyle travellers: Backpacking as a way of life', *Annals of Tourism Research*, vol. 38, no. 4, pp. 1535–1555. doi:10.1016/j.annals.2011.02.002

Coles, T., Hall, M.C. and Duval, D.T. 2009. 'Post-disciplinary tourism'. *In*: J. Tribe, ed. *Philosophical issues in tourism*. Bristol: Channel View Publications, pp. 80–100.

Colman, F. 2007. 'Affective Intensity: Art as sensorial form'. *In*: B. Bolt, F. Colman, G. Jones, and A. Woodward, eds. *Sensorium: Aesthetics, art, life*. Newcastle: Cambridge Scholars Publishing, pp. 64–83.

Crang, M. 1999. 'Knowing, tourism and practices of vision'. *In*: D. Crouch, ed. *Leisure/tourism geographies: Practices and geographical knowledge*. London and New York: Routledge, pp. 238–256.

Crouch, D. 2004. 'Tourist practice and performances'. *In*: A. Lew, C. Hall and A. Williams, eds. *A companion to tourism*. Malden, MA: Blackwell, pp. 85–95.

Currie, R.R., Campbell-Trant, T. and Seaton, S. 2011. 'Joining the in-crowd: Symbols for backpacker identity', *International Journal of Culture, Tourism and Hospitality Research*, vol. 5, no. 1, pp. 47–56. doi:10.1108/17506181111111753

DeLanda, M. 2006. *A new philosophy of society: Assemblage theory and social complexity*. London and New York: Continuum.

Deleuze, G. and Guattari, F. 2004. *A thousand plateaus: Capitalism and schizophrenia*, trans. B. Massumi. London: Continuum.

Dolphijn, R. and Van der Tuin, I. eds. 2012. *New materialism: Interviews and cartographies*. Ann Arbor: Open Humanities Press.

Edensor, T. 2007. 'Mundane mobilities, performances and spaces of tourism', *Social & Cultural Geography*, vol. 8, no. 2, pp. 199–215. doi:10.1080/14649360701360089

Elliott, A. and Urry, J. 2010. *Mobile lives*. London and New York: Routledge.

Franklin, A. 2003. *Tourism: An introduction.* London: Sage.

Franklin, A. 2014. 'On why we dig the beach: Tracing the subjects and objects of the bucket and spade for a relational materialist theory of the beach', *Tourist Studies*, vol. 14, no. 3, pp. 261–285. doi:10.177/1468797614536331.

Gren, M. and Huijbens, E.H. 2012. 'Tourism theory and the earth', *Annals of Tourism Research*, vol. 39, no. 1, pp. 155–170. doi:10.1016/j.annals.2011.05.009

Grosz, E. 2005. *Time travels: Feminism, nature, power*. Crows Nest: Allen and Unwin.

Grosz, E. 2008. *Chaos, territory, art: Deleuze and the framing of the earth*. New York: Columbia University Press.

Grosz, E. 2011. 'Matter, life, and other variations', *Philosophy Today*, vol. 55, pp. 17–27.

Haldrup, M. and Larsen, J. 2010. *Tourism, performance, and the everyday: Consuming the orient*. Oxon and New York: Routledge.

Hannam, K. and Ateljevic, I. eds. 2007. *Backpacker tourism: Concepts and profiles*. Clevedon: Channel View Publications.

Hollinshead, K. 2010. 'Tourism studies and confined understanding: The call for a "new sense" postdisciplinary imaginary', *Tourism Analysis*, vol. 15, no. 4, pp. 399–410. doi:10.3727/108354210X12864727693669

Hollinshead, K. and Ivanova, M. 2013. 'The multilogical imagination: Tourism studies and the imperative for postdisciplinary knowing'. *In*: M. Smith and G. Richards, eds. *Routledge handbook of cultural tourism*. Abingdon, Oxon and New York: Routledge, pp. 53–62.

Hui, A. 2012. 'Things in motion, things in practices: How mobile practice networks facilitate the travel and use of leisure objects', *Journal of Consumer Culture*, vol. 12, no. 2, pp. 195–215. doi:10.1177/1469540512446873

Ingold, T. 2010. 'Footprints through the weather-world: Walking, breathing, knowing'. *In*: T. Marchland, ed. *Making knowledge: Explorations of the indissoluble relation between mind, body, and environment*. Oxford: Wiley-Blackwell, pp. 115–132.

Jensen, M.T., Gyimothy, S. and Jensen, O.B. 2015. 'Staging interrail mobilities', *Tourist Studies*, Epub ahead of print. pp. 1–22. doi:10.1177/1468797615594740

Jensen, O.B. 2009. 'Flows of meaning, cultures of movement—Urban mobility as meaningful everyday life practice', *Mobilities*, vol. 4, no. 1, pp. 139–158. doi:10.1080/17450100802658002

Larsen, J. 2008. 'Practices and flows of digital photography: An ethnographic framework', *Mobilities*, vol. 3, no. 1, pp. 141–160. doi:1080/17450100701797398

Latour, B. 1990. 'Drawing things together'. *In*: M. Lynch and S. Woolgar, eds. *Representations in scientific practices*. Cambridge, MA and London: The MIT Press, pp. 19–68.

Latour, B. 1996. 'On Interobjectivity', *Mind, Culture, and Activity*, vol. 3, no. 4, pp. 228–245. doi:10.1207/s15327884mca0304_2

Latour, B. 2007. *Reassembling the social*. New York: Oxford University Press.

Latour, B. 2014. 'Agency at the time of the Anthropocene', *New Literary History*, vol. 45, no. 1, pp. 1–18. doi:10.1353/nlh.2014.0003

Law, J. 2002. *Aircraft stories: Decentering the object in technoscience*. Durham and London: Duke University Press.

Law, J. 2004. *Matter-ing: Or how might STS contribute?* Lancaster: Centre for Science Studies, Lancaster University. Retrieved 20 July 2016 from: www.lancaster. ac.uk/fass/resources/sociology-online-papers/ . . . /law-matter-ing.pdf

Law, J. and Hassard, J. eds. 1999. *Actor network theory and after*. Oxford: Blackwell Publishers.

Law, J. and Singleton, V. 2013. 'ANT and politics: Working in and on the world', *Qualitative Sociology*, vol. 36, no. 4, pp. 485–502. doi:10.1007/s11133-013-9263-7

Lean, G. 2012. 'Transformative travel: A mobilities perspective', *Tourist Studies*, vol. 12, no. 2, pp. 151–172. doi:10.1177/1468797612454624.

Lien, M.E. and Law, J. 2011. '"Emergent Aliens": On salmon, nature, and their enactment', *Ethnos: Journal of Anthropology*, vol. 76, no. 1, pp. 65–87. doi:10.1080/00 141844.2010.549946

Lonely Planet. 2016. *How to pack for any trip*. Carlton: Lonely Planet Publications Pty Ltd.

Lund, K.A. 2013. 'Experiencing nature in nature-based tourism', *Tourist Studies*, vol. 13, no. 2, pp. 156–171. doi:10.1177/1468797613490373

Manning, E. 2009. *Relationscapes*. Cambridge, MA: MIT Press.

Manning, E. 2010. 'Always more than one: The collectivity of *a Life*', *Body and Society*, vol. 16, no. 1, pp. 117–127. doi:10.1177/1357034X09354128

Manning, E. 2013. *Always more than one*. Duke University Press.

Marchland, T. ed. 2010. 'Introduction: Making knowledge: Explorations of indissoluble relation between mind, body, and environment'. *In: Making knowledge: Explorations of the indissoluble relation between mind, body, and environment*. Oxford: Wiley-Blackwell, pp. 1–20.

Merriman, P. 2014. 'Rethinking mobile methods', *Mobilities*, vol. 9, no. 2, pp. 167–187. doi:10.1080/17450101.2013.784540

Michael, M. 2000. 'These boots are made for walking . . .: Mundane technology, the body and human-environment relations', *Body and Society*, vol. 6, no. 3–4, pp. 107–126.

Mol, A. 2002. *The body multiple*. Durham: Duke University Press.

Mol, A. and Law, J. 1994. 'Regions, networks and fluids: Anaemia and social topology', *Social Studies of Science*, vol. 24, no. 4, pp. 641–671. doi:10.1177/ 030631279402400402

Mol, A. and Law, J. 2007. 'Embodied action, enacted bodies: The example of hypoglycaemia'. *In*: R.V. Burri and J. Dumit, eds. *Biomedicine as culture: Instrumental practices, technoscientific knowledge, and new modes of life*. London: Routledge, pp. 87–107.

Murphy, L. 2001. 'Exploring social interactions of backpackers', *Annals of Tourism Research*, vol. 28, no. 1, pp. 50–67.

The North Face. n.d. *The North Face: Shop: Equipment.* Retrieved 2 November 2016, from: www.thenorthface.com/shop/equipment

O'Sullivan, S. 2006. *Art encounters Deleuze and Guattari: Thought beyond representation.* Hampshire and New York: Palgrave Macmillan.

Palsson, G. 2013. 'Ensembles of biosocial relations'. *In*: T. Ingold and G. Palsson, eds. *Biosocial becomings: Integrating social and biological anthropology.* New York: Cambridge University Press, pp. 22–41.

Pearce, P. 1990. *The backpacker phenomenon: Preliminary answers to basic questions.* Townsville: Department of Tourism, James Cook University.

Picard, D. 2012. 'Tourism, awe and inner journeys'. *In*: M. Robinson, D. Picard and D. Ioannides, eds. *New directions in tourism analysis: Emotions in motion: Tourism, affect and transformation.* London: Routledge, pp. 1–20.

Picken, F. 2010. 'Tourism, design and controversy: Calling on non-humans to explain ourselves', *Tourist Studies*, vol. 10, no. 3, pp. 245–263. doi:10.1177/1468797611407757

Richards, G. and Wilson, J. eds. 2004. 'Drifting towards the global nomad'. *In*: *The global nomad: Backpacker travel in theory and practice.* Bristol, UK: Channel View Publications, pp. 3–13.

Sheller, M. and Urry, J. eds. 2004. 'Places to play, places in play'. *In*: *Tourism mobilities: Places to play, places in play.* London: Routledge, pp. 1–10.

Sørensen, A. 2003. 'Backpacker ethnography', *Annals of Tourism Research*, vol. 30, no. 4, pp. 847–867. doi:10.1016/S0160-7383(03)00063-X

Thrift, N. 2007. *Non-representational theory: Space, politics, affect.* London: Routledge.

Uriely, N., Yonay, Y. and Simchai, D. 2002. 'Backpacking experiences: A type and form analysis', *Annals of Tourism Research*, vol. 29, no. 2, pp. 520–538.

Urry, J. 2003. *Global complexity.* Malden, MA: Polity Press.

Urry, J. 2011. 'Does mobility have a future?'. *In*: M. Grieco and J. Urry, eds. *Mobilities: New perspectives on transport and society.* Ashgate, pp. 3–20.

Urry, J. and Larsen, J. 2011. *The tourist gaze 3.0.* London: SAGE Publication Ltd.

Van der Duim, R. 2007. 'Tourismscapes: An actor-network perspective', *Annals of Tourism Research*, vol. 34, no. 4, pp. 961–976. doi:10.1016/j.annals.2007.05.008

Van der Duim, R., Ren, C. and Jóhannesson, G.T. 2012. *Actor-network theory and tourism: Ordering, materiality and multiplicity.* London and New York: Routledge.

Veijola, S., Molz, J.G., Pyyhtinen, O., Höckert, E. and Grit, A. eds. 2014. 'Introduction: Alternative tourism ontologies'. *In*: *Disruptive tourism and its untidy guests.* Hampshire and New York: Palgrave Macmillan, pp. 1–18.

Walsh, N. and Tucker, H. 2009. 'Tourism "things": The travelling performance of the backpack', *Tourist Studies*, vol. 9, no. 3, pp. 223–239. doi:10.1177/146879 7610382706

Week, L. 2012. 'I am not a tourist: Aims and implications of "travelling"', *Tourist Studies*, vol. 12, no. 2, pp. 186–203. doi:10.1177/1468797612454627

3 Mobile-Spatial Encounters

The 'space' of packing is never isolated to the physical object of the bag or the designated geometric area of close proximity to the bag. The packing process encompasses a space that is beyond the perimeter of the bag, extending past the area on the bed or floor where the packing is happening (Figure 3.1). Spatial boundaries are set in motion through the movements of the packing process. Objects move in and out of the bag, we move in and out of rooms, around beds, and so on. As objects are located, collected, and moved into arrangements they spill out onto the floor or the bed, are strewn around the dormitory, and then collated and reassembled as they are moved

Figure 3.1 A bird's eye view of the dispersion of objects as a tourist is packing on the floor

back into the bag. In an interview, one traveller reflected about how much space they take up while packing: 'I open it up and take stuff out as I need it. I, err, sometimes I just throw it all out around the room, kinda, and then just work the way through it, but I'm real messy'.

Expanding and collapsing, distorting and producing space, the packing process requires movements within and across spatial boundaries, designations, constraints, and comfort zones (Figure 3.2). These are performances of 'not only people and objects, but also spaces' (Van der Duim 2007, p. 968). The result is a collaborative engagement with the surrounding actors through which multiple experiences of space arise from shifts in spatial qualities. Many of us will have experienced the messiness of packing that transforms our movements and alters the shared space we co-produce and co-inhabit. Whether we are in the privacy of our own homes, in a hotel room, or in a communal hostel dormitory room, our movements rearrange and disperse spatial qualities and boundaries. It can be difficult to negotiate piles of objects that will not fit neatly into a bag or articulate what went 'wrong' or why things did not go to plan. However, such moments are indicative of the constantly moving network of actors that we find ourselves within.

Experiences and engagements with spatiality are relational and fluid. Because of this, the lived experiences that arise through our engagement with space are separate, but always linked, to the concepts and perceptions

Figure 3.2 Six people's belongings intermingled in a hostel dorm room

of space. Doreen Massey suggests that '[w]e develop ways of incorporating a spatiality into our ways of being in the world' that respond to ideals, imaginations, and histories of spaces crafted from culture, imagination, and challenges of negotiating 'the enormous reality of space' (2005, p. 8). Exploring spatiality leads to further discussions and concerns of how spatialities congeal to become complex environments (see Chapter 4) and offer a way to understand practices of mobilities in tourism and daily transitions. Untangling the formal designation or perception of an area (space), the characteristics that may produce affects (spatial qualities), and the experience as we interact across various situations and sensations (spatiality), brings to the foreground the extent that our mobile-spatial encounters inform and alter networks of actors.

This chapter explores a number of issues related to mobile-spatial encounters that are experienced while packing. Mobile-spatial encounters influence our actions and decision-making processes that involve and draw upon other mobile systems within tourism and in everyday mobilities. In addition, aesthetic factors impinge upon this complex set of interactions, as do the particularities of individual and collective spatial experiences (spatialities). I begin by focusing on how tourists negotiate spatiality and forge new techniques of aligning and moving in mobile and turbulent encounters. Discussions of spatiality are positioned within the dormitory-style hostel rooms, where many people, objects, and architectural elements combine into a communal atmosphere, primed for the unexpected. Next, I examine how theories of spatial boundaries, compositions and aesthetics influence our packing decisions and routines. I hone in on the manner that global tourist cultures have imbued packing and planning with a spatial aesthetic, formed through the marketed ideals of technologies and materials to aid and assist our packing processes. However, this often stands in contrast to the actual, unexpected, or haphazard events that unfold in communal hostel spaces. In the final section, I show how spatiality is practiced in tourism situations, that is, through the formation of formulaic and attentive spatial practices of individuals, to the more fluid and relational movements that are set into motion via networks of actors.

Packing in Communal Hostelling Spaces

Tourism contributes to the growing attention to movement across vast and growing spaces, and as such it is important to link practical and theoretical engagement across a multitude of spatial experiences. The theoretical shift from analysis of stationary or fixed actors or phenomena to the mobilised relations across spaces embraces a ' "wayfaring" perspective [that] stresses movement both in terms of the many vicissitudes and sensory registers of travel-encounter' (Thrift 2006, p. 141). Whether fixed geographical locations or idealised destinations, spatial processes underpin many discussions and perceptions of tourism mobilities. The fluidity of global networks and actors (Mol and Law 1994, 2007; Urry 2003) implies that spatial configurations and the ongoing movement of human and nonhuman actors can create transgressions of habitual boundaries, forging new topological and spatial relations. Increased awareness of the entangled mobilities that span local and global situations means that 'what counts as "we" is being redefined', and, consequently, the 'number of actors' spaces that can be recognised and worked with' increases (Thrift 2007, p. 17). Therefore, it is necessary for mobilities research to be aware of how communal encounters are embedded in 'meanings and tasks' that 'are attributed to and distributed among people and things' (Van der Duim 2007, p. 962). Recognising nonhuman agency redraws the boundaries of human action, which implies that our movements negotiate ongoing relationships with other people, actors, and spaces.

Experiences of space are altered with every movement and are susceptible to subjective interpretations, socialised procedures, and everyday practices (Lefebvre 1991). Spatial negotiations and encounters are brought to the foreground when actions do not go to plan and our intended movements unravel in unexpected ways. Hostelling accommodation provides a unique way to study the collective and communal mobile-spatial encounters in tourism. The intensified, communal, and shared facilities mean that often guests are pushed out of their comfort zones. Rather than thinking and acting primarily for their own individual purposes, they must fit into a collective and co-constructed social space. They are unfamiliar spaces of 'encounter' that require 'a practical way of knowing' that 'entails a subtle set of negotiations around our bodies . . . and their habits' (Jack and Phipps 2005, p. 99). Hostels are prevalent in almost all areas in the world, and these low-budget, mostly shared accommodation spaces play into the ideals of the 'global nomad' (Richard and Wilson 2004) of being able to travel anywhere with relative ease. Hostels form part of the 'institutional infrastructure' that enables tourists to traverse geographical, cultural, and spatial mobilities (O'Regan 2010, p. 88). Far from the horror stories perpetuated in media and anecdotes, most hostels are clean and comfortable yet modest in their provisions for guests, generating tourist encounters that co-construct shared social spaces.[1]

Social interaction is a key motivator for choosing to stay in a hostel, and from my own experiences, this is also a factor for staying in communal hostel dormitories rather than a single, isolated room. Hostels perpetuate the backpacker 'symbol' and identity, and are considered as an essential part of the backpacking experience (O'Regan 2010). Laurie Murphy emphasises that interactions that develop in hostel social spaces are 'an integral and functional aspect of backpacking' (2001, p. 51). While some hostels fit within the notion of backpacker enclaves (Cohen 2004; Richards and Wilson 2004; Wilson and Richards 2008), the way that tourists might select accommodation often goes beyond the social status, image, or location of a hostel. The tourists that I spoke with were travelling for an assortment of reasons and motivations, from the leisure and holidaying tourists, younger students on study break, low-budget round-the-world travellers, or retirees, families, migrant workers, conference attendees, academics, artists—the list goes on (see Chapter 1). Such a diverse range of people implies that those who stay in hostelling accommodation are a heterogeneous group and do not necessarily fit within the 'backpacker' archetype (Hannam and Ateljevic 2007; Sørensen 2003).

Throughout this research, I stayed in large mixed dorms (male and female guests), sleeping side-by-side with the other guests in bunk beds (Figures 3.3 and 3.4). In most of the hostels I have stayed in (during research and in previous trips) the beds are arranged along the sides of the walls, and in the middle of the room is an open floor space where people can spread out their belongings. People often use the central floor space for packing, as well as social activities such as sharing a few drinks, playing cards, or studying maps and tourist pamphlets. The large global network of national hostel organisations, *Hostelling International*, promotes hostelling accommodation as the 'ideal for meeting new people' and prides their network's hostels on

Figure 3.3 A hostel dormitory in Kathmandu, Nepal

Figure 3.4 A hostel dormitory in Reykjavík, Iceland

providing communal spaces and 'facilities such as a common room, a self-catering kitchen, bar, restaurant, library, TV room, laundry facilities', and so on (Hostelling International 2016). In addition, it is common for hostels to market themselves as environmentally conscious organisations that encourage guests to recycle, share, and swap belongings and left over food in the communal areas (Figures 3.5 and 3.6). The emphasis on communal areas is significant in the way that hostels are marketed and desired by tourists.[2] The hostel atmosphere plays an important role in the kinds of expectations and perceptions of the travel experience for many tourists (Murphy 2001; O'Regan 2010). Many tourists I spoke with named the access to communal spaces, as well as the social atmosphere of the hostel, as the reason that they had chosen to stay in a hostel rather than a hotel or guesthouse.

The challenges, uses, and negotiation of communal and shared spaces in hostels came across in many of the interviews. The architectural design of the communal dorm rooms altered the way that people packed and stored their belongings (Figure 3.7). For instance, most tourists said that they used the lockers available in hostels (which were either in lockable cabinets in the dorm rooms, or in a separate 'locker room'). Several tourists commented that their individual bunk bed was a space that was fundamental for ensuring that they had organised themselves and their belongings. One tourist said she was constantly shifting her belongings around the room, describing that she would, 'take it out' of her bag, 'take it to my bed [laughs]

Figure 3.5 Views of the communal spaces in the hostel in Kathmandu, Nepal: the communal bar and rooftop area (left); author's belongings stored in the communal 'locker room' (right)

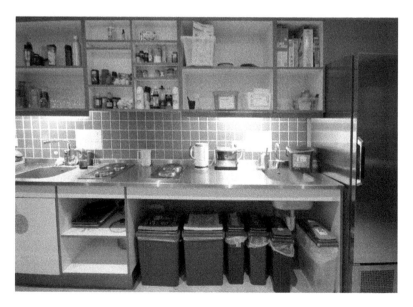

Figure 3.6 Communal kitchen area with free food shelves in a hostel in Reykjavík, Iceland

Figure 3.7 A tourist unpacking and sorting belongings on a table in the hostel's bar area

and it's on my bed. Then in the evening I take it back into the backpack'. In my own experiences staying in shared spaces, I was also conscious about where my belongings were stored, or if they were in the way of other guests. I actively tried to document and keep track of my packing process each day, sketching in my journal the arrangement of objects in my bag and the hostel space (Figure 3.8; see also Barry 2016). The constant to and froing of materials, checking, moving, rearranging, and repositioning demonstrates that the packing process encompasses a much wider spatial area than the bag's perimeter, and responds to the communal space. Negotiating the communal and shared spaces in hostels also presents packing as a much more rigorous, durational activity.

Another tourist explained, 'when it's time to leave, if there's nothing on my bed and nothing in my locker, I'm pretty sure I've got everything'. Others described methods they used to keep their valuables stored in specific spaces in the hostel, with one tourist describing:

> I put most of my stuff, like, I probably put half of my money, away in the locker, and my passports, tickets, all that sort of stuff . . . I'd just thrown them in there not to have them floating around the place.

The idea of organising, sorting, and keeping tabs on where personal items are located might arise from fear of theft or belongings being borrowed and used, or simply misplacing items. The constant checking on how they have

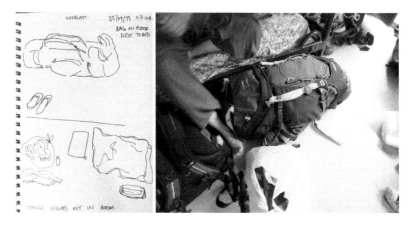

Figure 3.8 A sketch from my journal of the position of objects in my bag and spread out in the hostel room (left); photograph of myself at the completion of that day's packing and sorting (right)

stored things, or the spaces that they unpack their belongings into, was a recurring theme. These minute, fleeting actions, of being attentive to how we organise ourselves and our belongings by ensuring that our things are not 'floating around the place', seems critical in maintaining a harmonious, considerate, and shared space. This awareness of the spatial distribution of objects is indicative of how we co-construct relationships between ourselves in space and in relationship to other tourists and nonhumans, too.

The shared space of hostel dormitory rooms provides the perfect atmosphere for unpredicted events to unfold. For instance, in Kathmandu I had arranged to interview a tourist while he was packing to depart Nepal, after spending several months travelling the country. He said to meet him in the locker room where he would be packing his bag, which is a sparse room filled with built-in lockers on each wall and a small table in the centre of the room. Frequently people used the locker room to do their 'final pack' before flying out of Nepal, or before embarking on long trekking trips. It was common to find someone in the locker room taking up all of the floor space, so that anyone who wanted to access their own locker had to walk over and around another person's belongings. On this occasion, I was confronted with a sweet aroma as I entered the locker room. The tourist I had arranged to meet had spread his entire belongings out in the locker room (Figure 3.9). He explained:

> the reason I've spread it out is because I had honey spill everywhere, so . . . [trails off while he looks around the room] Yeah, this *little* jar of

Figure 3.9 A tourist re-packing in the communal locker room after honey had spilt through his bag

honey, and somehow it was protected like this, put here, kind of thing [mimes wrapping the jar up in other objects] so this doesn't break, it's pretty tough. Somehow it got loose, and. . . . [laughs] honey is runny, I didn't notice that [laughing]

He had bought the honey several months earlier and had been travelling around with it tightly wrapped in his backpack, until just then, when the jar had come open. The honey—a nonhuman actor—held the most agency in this haphazard situation. It reshaped the spatial boundaries of his packing process and altered the atmosphere of this hostel communal area. The entire locker room filled with the aroma of honey as he packed, breaching the usual proximities of packing. The honey would always be infused in the packing process as it covered most of his belongings with a sticky residue, even after he had washed items several times. As he moved objects around, more honey affixed itself to his belongings and the floor, and people walking in and out of the room had it stick to their shoes. The aroma infused all actors within this event. Days after he had left, the scent still lingered in the room. Relations were forged by the honey as it set in motion a different set of spatial experiences of packing for this tourist.

In these unexpected, haphazard moments, the relational and collective enactments of space are brought into focus. Such movements propel further movements, and collective action emerges, allowing the resonances of the situation to take hold. In such moments, a critical question is raised: if every*thing* is mobile, then our spatial encounters must be mobile, too. Therefore, how we navigate the flow of spatialities when we participate as tourists becomes the next issue. Travel magnifies situations that test our spatial perceptions and expectations, blurring, extending, and abstracting our attempts to align and orient within the complexity of movements within and across spatial qualities and collectively produced spatial experiences.

Unpacking Spatial Encounters

Space is difficult to talk about without falling into popular and general assumptions involving geometric areas and boundaries or competing scientific definitions. Designated geometric coordinates form a distinctive representation of space while boundaries within space are forged through habitual measurements. However, as Henri Lefebvre comments, 'space is constituted neither by a collection of things or an aggregate of (sensory) data, nor by a void packed like a parcel with various contents' (1991, p. 27). Lefebvre's apt description of a void to be 'packed' is a useful image to expand the complex mobile-spatial encounters that tourists have while packing. For instance, when the notion of 'space' is applied to packing, space tends to be understood as the area of the bag to be filled; in other words, a material object that functions as a container, demarcating interior and exterior areas of space. This is a limited understanding that does not account for the myriad of interactions, movements, and sensations that are experienced when packing, or the communal atmosphere that emerges through our interactions.

Even when space is perceived as a container or 'dimension', Doreen Massey explains that spaces are 'just as humanly produced as is place' (2006, p. 2). I read her comment as reinforcing that the idea of space, or the production of spaces, is never isolated to a static lingering dimension; rather, space is something processual and able to facilitate action. Space might not always be tactile; however, this does not excuse an overlooking of the processual interactions that we have with spaces.

In order to focus on the spatial encounters that tourists have, and how these lived experiences are co-constructed events, there needs to be a greater awareness of the affective experiences of space to allow us to move between and redraw spatial and material boundaries. Spatial experiences are 'always mobile and shifting across boundaries' and perceptions (Barry 2015, p. 10) and are often 'akin to the spatio-temporal regularities of everyday experience' (Edensor 2007, p. 200). However, as Tim Edensor cautions, these daily tasks and routine movements might also hold 'opportunities for transcending the banal' (2007, p. 200) that can be indicative of the complexities of how we shift across and respond to mobile-spatial encounters. For example, during an interview a tourist had rigorously packed everything into their suitcase, fitting objects into the bag with ease. As it was zipped closed, he realised that he had left out a large boxed bottle of whisky. 'This was going too well', he exclaimed, laughing. The whisky had been hidden from his view, placed behind him as he kneeled in front of the suitcase. 'Oh my god, this is so not going to close!' he said, laughing more as he fumbled with the bulky overflowing suitcase. The bag was packed tightly. He had expertly arranged the objects with few gaps between them, little space to spare. Yet an overseen object—a whisky bottle—now meant that he had to decant most of the objects from the suitcase.

In this instance, the bag was a void to be filled—a spatial container—and also an area that was filled with potential configurations of materials. We both laughed at this 'mishap' as he re-packed, taking considerably longer time to fit it all back in. A miscalculation, due to a single object being overlooked. However, you can extrapolate from this example the many ways that objects can be positioned where spatial demarcations—interior and exterior—are crossed and altered. This example in packing seems ready-made for Gaston Bachelard's theories on spatial boundaries (1994), since objects are never fixed into a specific spatial containment due to the boundaries constantly being shifted and altered. Bachelard suggests that 'objects *that may be opened*' have the potential to transform our perceptions of inside and outside boundaries because 'from the moment . . . [it] is opened, dialectics no longer exist . . . for the reasons that a new dimension—the dimension of intimacy—has just opened up' (1994, p. 85, original emphasis).

Attention to the interior and exterior boundaries demonstrates how contested and loaded spatial designations can be, and how problematic they can be during the packing process. Such encounters are indicative of the adaptive and generative practices that we perform in both tourism and in everyday routines. Many of the interviews with tourists entailed discussions of their bags as interior spaces, where the bags act as materialised spatial boundaries creating interior dimensions to contain objects. Comments such as 'I pretty much know where every item is in the backpack' or 'however I can make things fit, that's usually how they go into the suitcase' reinforce the idea of the bag as a spatial container to be filled. Tourists spoke of packing things *in* their bags or fitting things *inside*. Despite the obvious connotations of the task of containing objects within a bag, in general, the activity and movements carried out during the packing process do not always stick within these spatial designations. Miscalculating the capacity of a bag outlines the way in which one specific material artefact has the potential and ability to instigate a recalibration of boundaries. The examples from the interviews reveal how decision-making is often based on the aesthetics of spatial qualities and affects. Shifting across interior and exterior boundaries demonstrates how relations are constantly negotiated due to the spatial representations, experiences, and ideals.

Being active in organising ourselves within certain spatial arrangements can also involve shifts in scale. Moving across scales is symptomatic of travelling; tourists are constantly repositioning themselves within large flows of people, objects, and material-technological infrastructures. Movements 'coalesce into a series of macro- and micro-connected itineraries' (Fuller and Harley 2004, p. 44) as tourists negotiate their placement and arrangement in each new situation. Awareness of the shifting movements across scales is not always prominent because often technologies aid and smooth the experience of such shifts. The following example from an interview demonstrates shifts across scales: what is exterior space surrounding one object can also be an interior space of a larger object. The scale of the object and its proximity to other objects contributes to the multiplicity of spatial boundaries that are negotiated while packing. A tourist I interviewed used 'organising sacks' within their backpack (Figures 3.10 and 3.11), and explained how the interior space of their backpack was organised:

> I've got these, they're not compression sacks, just organising sacks, that I throw all my clothes into. They create nice neat little blocks. And then I basically try to pack everything in as a block, and then

Figure 3.10 The backpack with green organising sacks

Figure 3.11 The organising sacks being packed into the backpack

whatever's left on top. . . . they take up the entirety of the vertical or horizontal [space] that they're in. So in that way . . . everything fits in. . . . in tetris style.

The description of these organising sacks portrays them as compartmentalising objects, at once containing smaller objects yet simultaneously functioning as an object *to be packed* interior to the larger backpack. Although suitcases have had built in compartments and zippered segments that can be sealed off, this was the first time I had ever seen or heard of them. Within a few months of this interview, I began to see organising sacks for sale, designed and marketed to not only suitcase users, but also people using hiking backpacks (and yes, I bought some myself). Switching between singular objects (to be packed) and multiple objects (opening and containing smaller objects), the organising sacks designate spaces (interior and exterior) across a range of scales.

Figure 3.12 illustrates some of the issues of mobile-spatial practices that interior and exterior spaces take part in defining. Forming a multiplicity of arrangements of exterior space, the 'exteriors' cross scales of what is exterior to either the singular objects or collective objects (as unified and 'packed' into an organising sack). Technologies that are specific to packing, such as the organising sacks, smooth and alleviate any difficulties we might have negotiating materials, drawing attention to the multiple effects and enactments of each object. They momentarily stabilise and form clear

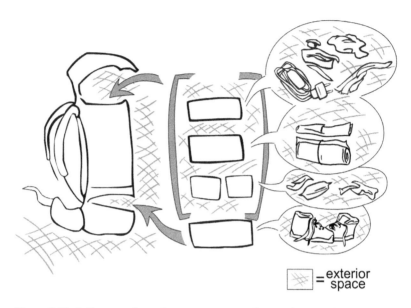

$\boxed{\times\!\!\times}$ = exterior space

Figure 3.12 A diagram of exterior space across various scales: exterior to the bag, exterior to the organising sacks, and exterior to the individual objects

demarcations of actor-networks (Ren, Jóhannesson and Van der Duim 2012, p. 22), while simultaneously showing the consequences of our interrelated actions by affording different spatial scales that present new relationships. Scales, in this instance, might be measured against the size of the objects, the zips on the backpack, our hands, or our bodies-as-a-whole. What is noteworthy about the shifts in scales while packing is that our attention and perception of spatial scales and boundaries are always mobile, that is, we are not always measuring items against ourselves in human (body) scale. Because '[a]ctors continually change size' (Thrift 2007, p. 17), our own position within a collective of actors is also just as mobile and tenuous.

When we pack, filling the gaps in a bag often becomes a puzzle and turns into a task where the movements of bodies and objects are determined by the 'combination of . . . usefulness and space available', as one tourist described. 'See, it looks like I don't know what I'm doing, it's a mess, but it's all like totally under control', another tourist explained. Relationships form through proximities and spatial arrangements as the packing process develops into a practiced negotiation. Many tourists commented that their packing process had evolved as they undertook more frequent travel or travelled for longer durations. Reflecting on the arrangement of objects, one tourist remarked, 'I think for the last few months I've been more or less content with, ah, with where everything is'. These comments draw attention to the relations of objects that are forged by an attention to spatial proximities, rather than the usual focus on conscious decisions and ideals of how tourists *want* to arrange objects in their bags.

Spaces are alive and *act* (Massey 2006, p. 2). They are integral to how relations unfold. As actors, spatial experiences are malleable and, like any material or immaterial actor, are susceptible to re-forming relations through interaction. Oscillations from individual–local to collective–global experiences forge networks and relations through movement (Latour 2007, p. 172). As Massey notes, 'All is movement. "Multiplicity" requires that we negotiate our interrelatedness, for those intersecting trajectories may clash, contradict each other, nestle together . . . or require the long hard effort of establishing mutual comprehension' (2006, p. 2). A relational conception of spatial encounters extends Massey's notion of the ongoing construction of interrelatedness. Negotiating spatial relationships, whether in tourism scenarios or everyday encounters, become practice where habitual processes evolve, requiring careful unravelling of the entangled mobilities we find ourselves within.

Spatialising Movements

Relationships that emerge as a function of our movements change our expectations of the task at hand (packing) and emphasise the ability to negate and reposition spatial boundaries and actions. The packed bag, which designates a closed off interior space with clearly discernible exterior boundaries, changes when it becomes part of a spatialising activity. 'Spatialising' is an emergent state where spatial qualities (such as scale, texture, volume) are not fixed to a particular designated or discernible boundary. It is a process where limits and boundaries of space are not yet fixed, but are in the accrual of their possible relationships to each other. They are constructing space, or 'spatializing' (2011, p. 90, original emphasis), to draw from Brian Massumi. This articulation of spatialising from Massumi is helpful because it emphasises that experiences driven by attention to spatial boundaries are emergent and relational.

When an object, in this case a bag, is presented as a complete material entity in which the outside and inside 'are offset against each other as different regions defined by the boundary: they are spatialized' (Massumi 2011, p. 92). The difference between interior and exterior spaces—as I described earlier with the example of organising sacks—presents a fixed and spatialised boundary. Or, when a suitcase is zipped shut, we perceive it as a spatial container; it is a spatialised entity. However, when the bag is unpacked, objects are decanted and scattered around the hostel room, when a tourist hovers around trying to decide on what order to re-pack, it is in a process of spatialising.

Massumi examines the process of spatialising through an example of drawing the shape of an oval on a piece of paper (2011, p. 90). Drawing in black ink, he describes how a series of lines form together as a boundary and visual barrier that creates the figure of an oval. Each line overlaps with the others, so that together they form the black oval drawn on the white paper. He suggests that if we look at the lines on the page as a collective, not as individual lines, they converge and 'propagate an outline' that we see (Massumi 2011, p. 91). Yet, before the lines propagate, before our vision blurs them into one larger drawing of an oval on the page, each single line stands apart from the others, and apart from the white paper on which it is drawn. This difference between black and white that we see, between the materials of the ink and paper, creates limits in which the drawing of the oval ceases to exist. These limits are not yet spatial, since it is in the accrual of their possible relationship to each other that they are constructing space or spatialising (Massumi 2011, p. 90). In the same way, the already spatialised bag, which designates closed-off interior and exterior boundaries, changes when it becomes part of a spatialising activity. When we are packing, the bag—in negotiation with the objects placed within it and the body packing—shifts between interior-exterior spatial parameters. The focus is no longer on the movement of objects as singular entities in space per se. Instead, attention shifts to the movements occurring in the spaces being forged through relations between actors.

As materials move and are moved, they open and flex spatialities and find themselves in a process of collaboration, moving with each other, forming and reforming. These spatialising events blur the boundaries between the designated, expected consequences, the material or spatial arrangements, and the network of relations that guide mobile-spatial encounters. This can be a turbulent, haphazard process in which we hover in negotiation as a set of individual entities. In such moments, we are not quite spatialised or set in formation, but open to the potentiality of collective action. For example, a tourist endearingly recounted the turbulent process of packing they had witnessed while on a group hiking trip. The following anecdote illustrates the unexpected or unplanned events during packing, and the adaptive capacity that our practices can form:

> I met this guy . . . and he lost everything because he was so, you know, his personality, it's just the way he was . . . And he was packing, every-thing was maybe five meters from each other, like it had exploded everywhere on the grass [laughs] . . . He was just standing and looking

in his underwear, and he didn't know where everything was, and he was just trying to pack it. He said "I don't know how this happened, I have so much stuff!" And he lost everything [with emphasis] *I mean everything*! He didn't take care, he was a mess. It was really funny to see how he was packing. . . . We'd been waiting for him for two hours, and his packing just took over everything . . . for him, everything mattered, even a sock, or the camera. If he lost his sock he would be as devastated as if he lost his camera. But it happened all the time. He got used to losing a GoPro camera or that sock . . . it's just interesting to see how every little object had a certain effect on him.

The tumultuous packing process this tourist witnessed of their travel companion demonstrates an instance where the individual's subjective decisions are being shifted and overturned as the actions are distributed across all actors. In this example, the spatial boundaries of packing are far from rigid and fixed. Not quite to plan, not quite spatialised, but in the process of spatialising as actors interact with each other, setting the expectations askew. Agency is no longer isolated to an individual actor but is distributed across collective movements. In this situation, the tourist relinquishes control over action as they allow the bag and objects to hover in negotiation.

Situations such as these reposition our sense and awareness of our individual movements within larger assemblages of mobilities. The assortment of objects that have been carefully selected to travel with are all as important as the composures of materials that give rise to the situation, such as the architecture of the room, the furniture, the bag, and the body, too. It is the shift from singular to multiple, or specific to generic experiences, which alter our perception of spatial boundaries and produce new relationships. It is only after undertaking these movements across spatial qualities and boundaries that 'the collective [will] have enough room to collect itself again' (Latour 2007, p. 172). Individual subjective decisions are overcome through experiences that are more-than habitual perception. In this way, felt and sensed, movements have a

> Relation to the imperceptible . . . Perception can grasp movement only as the displacement of a moving body or the development of a form. Movements, becomings, in other words, pure relations of speed and slowness, pure affects, are below and above the threshold of perception.
> (Deleuze and Guattari 2004, pp. 280–281)

The potential for each object to exceed their expected forms and purposes means that our human actions are, at times, not the dominant agency, rupturing our intended actions. Losing a sock or a camera due to a lack of organisation and disarray might be a result of not being able to simultaneously attend to each individual object within the large assemblage of our belongings. In these instances, affect strikes us as our sensing and feeling of the relationships between ourselves and others intensifies. This 'process cannot be characterized as exclusively subjective or objective . . . It involves subjective qualities as directly as the objects provoking them, or with which they move' (Massumi 2015, p. ix). Objects slip in and out of our perception, operating at different thresholds of agency. How we come to understand these affective resonances might be through acknowledging alternative registers of movement.

Sensing movement in the moment creates spatial affects that intensify the relational aspects of our individual–collective encounters. Erin Manning's examination of 'how movement can be felt before it actualizes' (2009, p. 6) is useful in positioning the way that tourists use spatial encounters to create new affective experiences. She suggests that space can be created through relational movements as the actors react and reconfigure together, altering and expanding the spatial boundaries of that situation (Manning 2009, p. 15). For instance, movements *with* objects have the ability to activate 'experimentation and play by bringing together the pastness of experience (the object as we know it) and its futurity (the object-ecology in its novel unfolding)' (Manning 2013, p. 95). Manning uses the term 'choreographic objects' (2013, pp. 92–93) to describe situations where objects *invite* movements. She states, '[c]reative autonomous opportunities are more likely to happen when an event alters how you experience space' (2013, p. 91). Manning suggests that choreographic objects

> present themselves as part of an evolving ecosystem. They extend beyond their objectness to become ecologies for complex environments that propose dynamic constellations of space, time, and movement. These "objects" are in fact propositions co-constituted by the environments they make possible.
>
> (2013, p. 92)

Manning's point is that objects *may* hold and compose attention, which initiate collective movements where 'objects are . . . more force than form' (2013, p. 95). When an object captures our attention, dissolving the spatial proximities between ourselves and the object, or the boundaries of its material form, releasing it from its status of an artefact, affective relations take hold. This can be in the most mundane or the startling and unexpected instances, where the affectivity of the object eschews 'the normalizing and condensing conventions of narrative' (Bissell 2009, p. 96). The object repositions us in relation to it and the myriad of other actors and sensations that we become alert to.

The practice of packing presents a similar situation in which objects become choreographic, where a space is opened for the interplay between the objects being packed and the person that is packing them. These are mutually constructed movements. In such instances, the expectations and interactions are constantly altering networks of relations. These 'objects force us to think differently about the enactment' of material and spatial relationships (Bissell 2009, p. 96). It is when things *won't fit*, when objects leak, spill, are squashed, that is, they *do not act in the way that we expect them to*, that we are suddenly made aware of the ways space and material assemblages are always in motion. Rather than our actions creating 'idealized space' or producing '[s]pace as reassurance', as Georges Perec eloquently terms it (2008, p. 15), interactions compose our experiences and require adaptation of our processes, which never settle.

Movements compose and re-compose through networks of actors in transition. In moments when our expected actions are overturned by an object, the feeling of movement generates 'collective affects' (Anderson 2009, p. 80) that are atmospheric and move us in unanticipated ways. Ben Anderson describes 'atmospheres [that] are spatially discharged affective qualities that are autonomous from the bodies that they emerge from, enable and perish with' (2009, p. 80). When we become aware of the relations between ourselves, other objects, spaces that we share, and the processes of action that are unfolding, we can 'move beyond our own experience, when we get disoriented in the sound of the in-between, it is the movement that takes over' (Manning 2013, p. 83). There is caution. The 'conditions have to be right for this to occur . . . When the body is no longer a container for movement but a force for the transduction of movement-moving, we will have gone beyond our own experience' (Manning 2013, p. 83). It is helpful—although difficult—to consider ourselves beyond our own immediacy of experience, beyond our individual subjective decisions and actions, and become aware of the collective movements that are composing.

I am proposing that if approached in a certain way, everyday practices such as packing a bag can intensify our attunement to spatial affects and become practices that can be applied elsewhere in daily life. Attention to the potentiality of material agency results in movements and relationality that reposition individual ideals and expectations of how we position and locate ourselves, and may value other forms of experience. So, how is a person affected by an event not registered as a single, isolated occurrence of an individual body? Annemarie Mol and John Law observe that '[w]hile a body-in-practice may incorporate some of its surroundings it may also . . . excorporate some of its actions. The very activity of intra-sensing may take place outside one's body-proper' (2007, p. 96). Although a single person might initiate an action, the movements are not isolated to the body or the objects in immediate proximity. Feeling and sensing can become dispersed across multiple spatial locales enacted as a collective experience: for instance, the body's position, the surrounding architecture, the proximity of other actors. We are 'being reconfigured' as our bodies, actions, and ideas are 'scattered' and 'distributed' (Urry 2016, p. 15). Subsumed into the collective situations and systems, John Urry reminds us that 'Individuals thus exist beyond their private bodies, leaving traces of themselves in space' (2016, p. 15). It is through collective actions that we shift our expectations as we respond to larger sets of movements that are happening.

Coordinating Spatialities

Movements that are undertaken during packing are embedded within a complex system of mobilities that transform with each interaction. Relations emerge and dissolve. Some assist in orienting us, and others feed back into the complexity of collaborative movements. It is only when we become aware of the fragility and malleability of relationships that we can interact with the fluidity of spatial boundaries that push materials (including ourselves) into new, collaborative processes.

Mobile-spatial encounters respond to touristic ideals, globalised cultures of mobilities, and our own habitual or regimented movements. It is a constant oscillation across scales of individual action and collective mobilities. The technologies and materials that assist and enable us to be on the move play a vital role in forming experiences that respond to constraints and conditions. They might be high-tech multi-component materials, or they can be more mundane, overlooked technologies that aid our transit and mediate relationships between bodily sensations and the environment (Michael 2000; Urry 2016; Walsh and Tucker 2009). As we 'navigate backwards and forwards between directly sensing the external world' while we 'move bodily in and through it', an array of 'objects and mundane technologies facilitate . . . kinaesthetic sense as they sensuously extend human capacities' (Urry 2016, p. 48). Regardless of the 'sophistication' of the materials or technologies, it is the manner in which they enable us to participate in networks actors as we move. With each movement, new collaborations between human and nonhumans are formed and reformed. 'There is always an element of "chaos". This is the chance of space' (Massey 2005, p. 111). Action is never isolated but always bound to the potential for new spatial encounters.

Communal situations, such as the shared social space of the hostel dormitory, emphasise that actions are never isolated but always in relation with others. Tourist practices insist on being attentive to such 'chance' and harnessing these potentials. Experiences that transcend expectations and preconceptions disrupt and unsettle us, but can be indicative of unexpected yet affective experiences. The congealing of socio-cultural, material, and spatial influences and ideals requires collaboration and adaptation. Shifting across scales of movement requires adaptive and generative practices that connect and ground our actions to an array of actors. The question of 'how to position ourselves "in the middle" of these shifting networks' (Ren et al. 2012, p. 19) is an ongoing uncertainty that prompts new formations of mobile practices.

The way that spatial qualities and boundaries influence our intended and actual actions goes beyond the practice of packing and can be applied in a realm of other examples in daily life. Whether as a tourist who is travelling for leisure, a researcher tracing mobile experiences, or a person who is bound up in the bustle of the mundanity of everyday tasks, spatial negotiations are invariably complex and communal encounters. In packing, spatial processes are emblematic of routinised movements that require adaptations of space available and desired outcomes (such as filling the bag and zipping it closed), but are also indicative of the processual engagements that we draw on to create knowledge and experience from. It signals how practices can and do move beyond being just an everyday routine toward a honed practice of negotiating spatialities and mobilities that operate at various scales and intensities. At times these might be more contemplative or conceptual strategies for aligning ourselves within specific spatial constraints, while in other instances it might be a more haptic and ad-hoc approach where we move re-actively. Regardless of how large or small, negotiating spatial qualities and boundaries generates new connections, understandings, and practice-led experiences that are devised to enable us to move individually and collectively.

Notes

1 Generally, most hostels offer a variety of accommodation options, such as large communal dormitory rooms with bunk beds (10+ beds in one room, with a communal bathroom), smaller dormitory rooms for either single or mixed sexes (4–6 beds), and private rooms for individuals, families, couples, or small groups. The price is indicative of the amount of space and facilities that you share. A notable point is that most hostels charge slightly more for beds in 'all female' dormitory rooms. In addition, some hostels have an 'age limit' (usually 30 or less), fitting into the tradition of 'youth hostelling' (though this is now quite rare), and other hostels require guests to become a member of their network or association.

2 Although two of the hostels that I conducted research in were members of the Hostelling International network (Reykjavík Downtown and Reykjavík Loft), the others were not. However, all hostels that I stayed in while collecting data did provide similar communal facilities and all were rated very highly on websites such as 'hostelworld.com' and 'booking.com'.

References

Anderson, B. 2009. 'Affective atmospheres', *Emotion, Space and Society*, vol. 2, no. 2, pp. 77–81. doi:10.1016/j.emospa.2009.08.005

Bachelard, G. 1994. *The poetics of space*. Boston: Beacon Press.

Barry, K. 2015. 'The aesthetics of aircraft safety cards: Spatial negotiations and affective mobilities in diagrammatic instructions', *Mobilities*, first published online before print: 2 Nov, 2015. doi:10.1080/17450101.2015.1086101

Barry, K. 2016. 'Diagramming: A creative methodology for tourist studies', *Tourist Studies*, first published online before print: Nov 28, 2016. doi:10.1177/1468797 616680852

Bissell, D. 2009. 'Inconsequential materialities: The movements of lost effects', *Space and Culture*, vol. 12, no. 1, pp. 95–115. doi:10.1177/1206331208325602

Cohen, E. 2004. 'Backpacking: Diversity and change. *In*: G. Richards and J. Wilson, eds. *The global nomad: Backpacker travel in theory and practice*. Bristol, UK: Channel View Publications, pp. 43–59.

Deleuze, G. and Guattari, F. 2004. *A thousand plateaus: Capitalism and schizophrenia*, trans. B. Massumi. London: Continuum.

Edensor, T. 2007. 'Mundane mobilities, performances and spaces of tourism', *Social & Cultural Geography*, vol. 8, no. 2, pp. 799–215. doi:10.1080/14649360701360089

Fuller, G. and Harley, R. 2004. *Aviopolis: A book about airports*. London: Black Dog Publishing.

Hannam, K. and Ateljevic, I. 2007. 'Introduction: Conceptualising and profiling backpacker tourism'. *In: Backpacker tourism: Concepts and profiles*. Clevedon: Channel View Publications, pp. 1–8.

Hostelling International. 2016. 'Hostels FAQs', *Hostelling International*. Retrieved 13 December 2016 from: www.hihostels.com/pages/hostels-faqs

Jack, G. and Phipps, A. 2005. *Tourism and intercultural exchange: Why tourism matters*. Clevedon, Buffalo and Toronto: Channel View Publications.

Latour, B. 2007. *Reassembling the social*. New York: Oxford University Press.

Lefebvre, H. 1991. *The production of space*, trans. D. Nicholson-Smith. Oxford: Blackwell Publishers Ltd.

Manning, E. 2009. *Relationscapes*. Cambridge: MIT Press.

Manning, E. 2013. *Always more than one*. Durham, NC: Duke University Press.

Massey, D. 2005. *For space*. London: Sage Publications Ltd.

Massey, D. 2006. 'Moving spaces'. *In*: E.H. Huijbens and Ó.P. Jónsson, eds. *Sensi/able spaces: Space, art and the environment*. Proceedings of the SPARTEN conference, Reykjavík, June 1st and 2nd, 2006. Newcastle: Cambridge Scholars Publishing, pp. 2–5.

Massumi, B. 2011. *Semblance and event: Activist philosophy and the occurrent arts*. Cambridge, MA: MIT Press.

Massumi, B. 2015. *Politics of affect*. Cambridge: Polity.

Michael, M. 2000. 'These boots are made for walking . . .: Mundane technology, the body and human-environment relations', *Body and Society*, vol. 6, no. 3–4, pp. 107–126.

Mol, A. and Law, J. 1994. 'Regions, networks and fluids: Anaemia and social topology', *Social Studies of Science*, vol. 24, no. 4, pp. 641–671. doi:10.1177/030631 279402400402

Mol, A. and Law, J. 2007. 'Embodied action, enacted bodies: The example of hypoglycaemia'. *In*: R.V. Burri and J. Dumit, eds. *Biomedicine as culture: Instrumental practices, technoscientific knowledge, and new modes of life*. London: Routledge, pp. 87–107.

Murphy, L. 2001. 'Exploring social interactions of backpackers', *Annals of Tourism Research*, vol. 28, no. 1, pp. 50–67.

O'Regan, M. 2010. 'Backpacker hostels: Place and performance'. *In*: K. Hannam and A. Diekmann, eds. *Beyond backpacker tourism: Mobilities and experiences*. Bristol: Channel View Publications, pp. 85–101.

Perec, G. 2008. *The species of spaces and other pieces*, trans. J. Storrock. London: Penguin Books.

Ren, C. Jóhannesson, G.T. and Van der Duim, R. 2012. 'How ANT works'. *In*: R. Van der Duim, C. Ren and G.T. Jóhannesson, eds. *Actor-network theory and tourism: Ordering, materiality and multiplicity*. Oxon: Routledge, pp. 13–25.

Richards, G. and Wilson, J. eds. 2004. 'Drifting towards the global nomad'. *In: The global nomad: Backpacker travel in theory and practice*. Bristol, UK: Channel View Publications, pp. 3–13.

Sørensen, A. 2003. 'Backpacker ethnography', *Annals of Tourism Research*, vol. 30, no. 4, pp. 847–867. doi:10.1016/S0160-7383(03)00063-X

Thrift, N. 2006. 'Space', *Theory Culture Society*, vol. 23, no. 2–3, pp. 139–146. doi:10.1177/0263276406063780

Thrift, N. 2007. *Non-representational theory: Space, politics, affect*. Routledge.

Urry, J. 2003. *Global complexity*. Malden, MA: Polity Press.

Urry, J. 2016. *Mobilities*. Cambridge: Polity Press.

Van der Duim, R. 2007. 'Tourismscapes: An actor-network perspective', *Annals of Tourism Research*, vol. 34, no. 4, pp. 961–976. doi:10.1016/j.annals.2007.05.008

Walsh, N. and Tucker, H. 2009. 'Tourism "things": The travelling performance of the backpack', *Tourist Studies*, vol. 9, no. 3, pp. 223–239. doi:10.1177/146879 7610382706

Wilson, J. and Richards, G. 2008. 'Suspending reality: An exploration of enclaves and the backpacker experience', *Current Issues in Tourism*, vol. 11, no. 2, pp. 187–202. doi:10.2167/cit371.0

4 Moving With/in Environments

Many experiences that we have while we are mobile—whether in tourism situations or in our everyday routines and movements—are direct engagements with environments. Environments envelop us. Some we carry with us from our point of origin; others engulf us as we move into them. Environments are sets of organic and inorganic conditions such as the terrain, topography, climate, season, and weather, in addition to the human and nonhuman inhabitants. These conditions produce tangible experiences that arise through collaborative interactions. Altering our daily procedures through moments of re-orientation to new surroundings, the environment moves us and we move with the environment. Individual consumption practices are momentarily dispersed and modified by moving with the environment. Tourism provides exemplar situations where our actions are constantly re-adjusting and adapting to always being in transition and the new co-consumptive practices that arise.

The environmental conditions and aesthetics that we are bound within play an important role in enabling or restricting our movements and the formation of mobile experiences. These may be small and subtle adjustments to changes in weather or seasons, or it might be larger-scale re-orientations that respond to awe-inspiring environmental aesthetics that inform tourist desires and travel decisions. The experiences that tourists have within large, immersive landscapes highlight the numerous subtle negotiations with/in environmental conditions. By looking at the larger dynamic scale of actions that constitutes the environment, it is possible to observe the coordination of spatial and material interactions that occur across all actors in everyday practices. I am suggesting that the actions taken when engaging with environments facilitate alternative conceptions of collaborative, co-consumptive, and sustainable practices of tourism mobilities.

This chapter examines how certain tourist destinations intensify our awareness to moments of reorientation with/in environments and how this affects everyday processual interactions, specifically packing a bag. First,

I provide an understanding that we are part of the environment as a constant (re)composure with it through our movements. I use the term '(re) composure' to describe the transitions that assemble human and nonhuman actors into specific configurations of environmental conditions, which feed back into the environmental surround. After sketching out a definition of 'environment', I outline how we move with and re-orient ourselves with and through environments, reflexively analysing examples from my own experiences as a tourist and researcher. These moments are suggestive of reconfigured relationships with our surroundings, alternating between touristic expectations and the affective resonances of the environments we encounter. Next, recent discussions on movements with 'nature', landscapes, and space are used to explore how the environments in Nepal and Iceland prepare tourists for certain kinds of experiences to be consumed. Using examples of my own packing experiences, I describe the immersive character of environmental ideals and aesthetics, which altered the intended actions. Finally, what emerges from these discussions are the ways in which practices of collaboration and co-consumption arise from tourists' re-orientations with/in environments. It is important to tackle the shifting intricacies of composition—(re)composing—during environmental experiences, arguing that sustainable or perhaps low-impact tourist experiences can be achieved through heightened attention and awareness to movements with/in environments. In this way, the environment as an actor that subtly attunes tourists is foregrounded. Processes of consuming are dispersed and shift away from individualistic, anthropocentric ideals of the destination in favour of collaborative practices that feed back into co-consumptive and collaborative environmental interactions. This is seen in the packing process, albeit in subtle ways. I argue that in order to evaluate the potential of touristic environmental encounters, we need to move with the environment.

(Re)composing the Environment as an Actor

Large, immersive landscapes and turbulent climates present navigation and orientation challenges. As tourists find themselves positioned within areas of vastness, the ability to determine distance and scale are skewed. In these moments of skewed orientation, immersive experiences offer stark contrast to touristic expectations. A tourist's experience is often conditioned by pre-packaged ideals, expectations of what they will encounter and consume, and 'must-do' behaviours. Tourists consume experiences and in doing so form 'portfolios of cultural activities' (Warde 2005, p. 144). These consumptive patterns are made possible, as Alan Warde explains, through 'commitment to practices' (2005, p. 144), that is, practices of engagement with the intensities of their surrounds. Tourists' heightened sensory awareness amplifies subtle negotiations, working against the marketed consumption of idealised vistas or tourism rituals. Awareness of other modes of engagement and consumption transform usual or everyday tourism activities—such as exploring the destination on foot, in a tour, taking photographs, or packing bags— into moments of re-orientation that unfold through sensory engagements with and through the environment. Whether ritualised ideals mesh with the in-situ momentary sensations, or alternative ideals of consumption are found, people in-transit are not just mediated by the environment, but are in direct collaboration with it.

A broader conception of what constitutes an environment is required to examine the kinds of activities that tourists undertake *with* the environment. It is important to understand the environment as an actor and as a process of constant (re)composure. The 'environment' is not isolated to the geographical, cultural, or ecological attributes of the destination; rather, it is bound to us through experience, changing and altering with each movement. This understanding involves noticing how tourists adjust to a host of bodily and environmental shifts, including phenomenon such as jetlag (Anderson 2013; Waterhouse, Reilly, Atkinson and Edwards 2007) or oppositional climates and seasons, exacerbating the differences between points of departure and arrival. Often the 'interval between departure from the familiar to the point in time when one's own instincts of orientation kick in again' (Sverrisdóttir 2011, p. 82) prompts our individual preconceptions of the destination to fuse with our adjustments to unfolding events. The many ways that an environment is imagined, perceived, and then experienced is also shaped by a socio-cultural imaginary and formed through a 'history of interactions and influences' such as media, transit, geography, and situation encountered upon arrival (Lim 2008, p. 389).

We are 'always intermeshed with the more-than-human world' and 'inseparable from "the environment"' (Alaimo 2008, p. 238). If we accept that the environment is not external, that it forms 'regions of the body's very existence' (Ingold 2010, p. 116), then the environment can be understood as an actor that 'modifies' and makes 'a difference' to events (Latour 2007, p. 71). A new materialist perspective emphasises the material constitution of our bodies, opening up possibilities for us to be in composure with the environment through activities with actors that are greater than ourselves as individuals (see Alaimo 2008; Bennett 2010; Bryant 2011; Morton 2007). These reflections highlight the problematic of trying to distinguish where the environment ends and an individual body begins. In short, there is not always a clear boundary to how the environment shapes our bodily experiences and vice versa.

The haze, vastness, and scales of the destination skew our usual bodily alignments. We change as our surroundings change. Our new sensing of the environment composes with us a re-oriented sense of the destination that shifts our practices towards collaborative experiences of moving and transiting to be consumed. The environment, when freed up and considered no longer as an abstract spatial entity, becomes an unfolding of constant (re)composure through a multitude of entities and spaces: a networked, or relational, ecology.

Constantly refiguring and conditioning, we are always in direct connection with the environment. The artists-architects Arakawa and Madeline Gins use the term 'organism-person-environment' (Gins and Arakawa 2002, pp. 1–5) to describe an understanding of a person as a constant composition with the environmental surround. The actions that occur within any given event compose a range of actors that inseparably affect each other to shape the shared environment: the body, the architecture of the room, the geographical location, and the many objects in proximity. For Arakawa and Gins, the ' "environment" does not consist of unitized entities filling an external space' (Gendlin 2013, p. 222). Rather, an organism-person-environment is an 'integrally intelligent whole, always capable of bringing conscious reflection into the mix, the organism-person feels and thinks its (way through an) environment' (Gins and Arakawa 2002, p. 3).

If we accept that the environment is not an external, passive entity, but rather is an actor that is entangled through and across all other actors in the situation, then the ability to determine where a body begins and ends is an environmental question. This fundamentally alters the ways in which we consider tourism practices of consuming and producing mobilities and, in turn, can be used as a starting point for unravelling new approaches to touristic experiences.

Rosi Braidotti's 'nomadic theory' (2008, 2012) extends these concepts of environmental and bodily entanglements and affirmatively positions a body as *material* and bound through fluid reflexive movements with the environment (2008, p. 183; see Chapter 2). Braidotti's approach is to open up potential experiences that might become a sustainable nomadism that 'contest[s] the arrogance of anthropocentrism and strikes an alliance with the productive force of . . . life in its inhuman aspects' (2012, p. 139). In doing so, the subject is re-grounded and 'marked by interdependence with its environment' (Braidotti 2008, p. 182). Opportunities for collaborative experiences of humans and environments are presented, where subjectivities are understood as an affective resonance that develops between individual and collective experiences. Acknowledging the collective consumption of experience and the resulting collaborative practices requires attention to collective everyday (or touristic) practices (Warde 2005, p. 146).

These propositions, of nomadic, body-environments, or an organism-person-environment, acknowledge the material constitution of our bodies, illustrating that the boundaries between the individual human, nonhumans in the situation, and the environment are never isolated and are integrated through action. Extracting these points from a range of disciplines and theories, a definition begins to take form, if only momentarily. An environment: a melding of actions that span ourselves as humans, and the terrain, climate, culture, and so on, as nonhumans entering into an ecology of relations. Propositions of different configurations of environments illustrate that the boundaries between the individual tourist and the environment of the destination can never be considered in isolation. The environment, under this new conception of collaborative relationships, becomes an actor that subtly attunes tourists, shifting our practices towards collaborative experiences of transition and mobility.

Re-orienting Touristic Movements

In order to re-orient with environments and find prospective new relationships with our surroundings, it is important to examine how we understand environments and how that understanding (pre-orientation) prepares tourists for certain kinds of experiences. Notions of space, nature, and landscape are discussed in this section in order to examine how environmental qualities are presented and consumed by tourists.

When travelling to a destination that has unique landscapes, we often approach the idea of 'nature' with expectations of how we will act and be affected. However, the results are not always clear, considering how much agency can be attributed to the environment that we enter into. Katrín Lund (2013) characterises the relationship between tourists and the perception of a 'natural' environment as a lapse into nature/culture or subject/object dichotomies. Viewing perception in a positive light, as a mode of negotiation and orientation, I suggest that tourists co-compose with the environment and constantly re-orient and attune their perception to the unfamiliar situations. As a result a collaborative co-selection process is initiated that can lead to new co-consumptive actions.

The environment becomes a mode of unfolding in constant (re)composure of a multitude of entities, a networked ecology. In order to comprehend how environments can be freed-up, no longer an abstract spatial entity, it is important to examine how mobile and tourism experiences consider alternative practices of space. Having greater responsiveness to space permits a shift away from the presupposed containment of spaces (Thrift 2007) as isolated destinations, toward a relational spatiality that encompasses all actors, including environments. Timothy Morton (2007) points out that the logic of space is deeply embedded in and constraining of our ability to change in relation to an environment. Morton states that, '[i]n order to have an environment, you have to have a space for it; in order to have an *idea* of an environment, you need ideas of space' (2007, p. 11, original emphasis). Rather than considering the environment as an enveloping force that surrounds us, what is required is a 'loosening up [of] the spatial constraints' (Thrift in Bech, Borch and Larsen 2010, p. 96).

Nigel Thrift discusses the way spatial discourses have turned away from a separation of 'site' and 'movement' (2006, p. 141), which means that even when stationary we are always engaged with mobile processes in some manner. This shift from analysis of stationary or fixed actors or phenomena to the mobilised relations across spaces embraces 'movement within mobilities' where 'the quality of the connections across sensory sensitivity, perceptual systems, conceptual processes and situated information inflects, deflects or allows movements to flourish and take a particular trajectory' (Barry and Keane 2017, p. 69). It is at this point that the desire for ourselves to feel the affective intensities of each situation and to acknowledge we are in a 'process of transition' (Braidotti 2012, p. 41) takes hold. We are always engaging in 'processes which create and shape the individual and its surroundings simultaneously' (Ren, Jóhannesson and van der Duim 2012, p. 17). Whether fixed geographical locations or idealised destinations, the way that tourists move with and in environments involves a consideration of representations of space and how we are positioned within specific spatial assemblages that co-constitute an environment.

Conceiving of the environment as an actor connects the many actions performed by tourists with the environment of each destination and each location we find ourselves within. Thus, the actions that unfold between tourists and the environment are 'multi-sensory and smooth spatial experience[s]' (Sverrisdóttir 2011, p. 82), requiring the body to move through conflicting perceptual and experiential moments. The notion of 'smooth space' that Hildigunnur Sverrisdóttir elicits in tourism practices is a space that is 'vectoral, projective, or topological' (Deleuze and Guattari 2004, p. 399). Drawing from Gilles Deleuze and Felix Guattari, Sverrisdóttir suggests that smooth space is composing, fluid, and haptic, filled with potential and yet is 'useless as a base of systemization' (2011, p. 80). The philosophical proposition of smooth space invokes potential for new collaborative re-orientations that merge bodies, environments, and all actors in a situation. Alternative processes of consuming arise: collaborative, co-productive, dispersed consumption that can be interwoven back into new relationships and experiences.

Recent reflections on tourists' interactions with environments, in particularly notions of landscape aesthetics, suggest that tourists recalibrate the relations between bodies and environments. This is done in a number of ways. For instance, the scenic aspects of environments 'invite' and 'inspire' tourists (Huijbens and Benediktsson 2013), while descriptions of 'human-landscape encounters' unique to Iceland have been posited (Benediktsson and Lund 2010, p. 8) and natural phenomenon are said to attune us to 'a flow of sensation' (Lund 2013, p. 158). In this way, appreciation of land-scape encompasses new 'understanding[s] of both place and landscape as *events*, as happenings, as moments that will again be dispersed' (Massey 2006, p. 46, original emphasis). The immersive landscape environment sur-passes the geographical or geological formation of the terrain. It is fluid and momentary, bound to and driving forward environmental compositions.

Whether it is termed 'nature', landscape, or an environment, there is a collective assemblage of actors forged through a complex entanglement of agency. Morton suggests that the environment is 'a way of consider-ing groups and collectives—humans surrounded by nature, or in continuity with other beings' (2007, p. 17). He concurs with Bruno Latour, cautioning that 'the actual situation is far more drastically collective than that' (Morton 2007, p. 17).

It is important to note the similarities between the new materialist approach, where bodies and objects are comprised of active matter (Alaimo 2008; Braidotti 2012; Bennett 2010), and Morton's ecological ontology, which both overlaps and extends works by Latour (2007, 2010) and many others working in actor-network perspectives (Barad 2007; Lien and Law 2011; Law and Singleton 2013; Van der Duim, Ren and Jóhannesson 2012; see also Chapter 2). Although these approaches differ in terminology, they share a preference for the distribution of material agency through action that transgresses human and nonhuman boundaries. Latour also warns that the end of nature is through ecology, as nature (in a modern sense) is 'a way of organizing the division . . . between appearances and reality, subjectiv-ity and objectivity, history and immutability' (2010, p. 476). What Latour is describing, and what Morton also points out, is that agency should not be divided up between human and nonhuman actions, but rather through momentary compositions (Latour 2010).

What this means for environmental encounters—whether in tourist ideals or in our everyday actions—is that all actions from all actors are collab-oratively negotiated. This mix of theoretical propositions and observa-tions highlights how tourists interact with a realm of other actors (persons, objects, or elements) that comprise an environment, in ways that are bound through mutual action that prompt a constant (re)composure of experience. Thus, the environment is never separate from our bodies; we collectively produce, interact, and co-consume with the environment. It moves with us as we move with it.

Navigating this complexity of heightened sensations and affects becomes a practice of re-orientation that seeps into and across mundane and everyday habits and routines, unsettling and altering our movements. The experience of being out on a tour looking at an erupting volcano feeds back into and resonates through our activities afterwards (see Chapter 1). These are affective situations that resonate through ourselves and surroundings (see Figure 4.1). The activities of registering, processing, and then re-orienting to multi-sensory and collective awareness are a delicate balancing act, informing future expectations and consumptions of tourist experiences.

In Nepal and Iceland, it was common to feel the preconceptions of the environment being confirmed or challenged, in my own experiences and also witnessing this tension in the actions of other tourists. For instance,

Figure 4.1 Photograph of the sunset taken outside a hostel window just after midnight (top); packing in Northern Iceland at 00:36am, with only ambient light filtering in through the window (bottom)

when walking down the street of downtown Reykjavík, I saw a group tourists pausing to look at the 'volcanic-looking' rocks that formed the footpath and kerbside. 'I wonder if they're from that volcano that erupted', I heard one tourist exclaim as he took photographs of the footpath (Figure 4.2). Similarly, in Nepal the proliferation of the colourful Tibetan prayer flags through urban and rural areas was a common talking point for tourists. 'I tried to jump up and grab them from a tree, just to touch them, but they were too high up', I heard one guy say in a bar. These iconic, touristic, and material entities divert our intended actions and, at times, push us into inquisitive and haphazard interactions. Materials (such as the 'volcanic-looking' rocks or the Tibetan prayer flags) resonate an idealised aesthetic that contributes to the perception of the environment tourists expect to encounter. The experiences of and interactions with such materials feed into the sensations that tourists expect to see, touch, feel, and consume. Following Warde's influential exploration of consumption and theories of practice (2005), Allison Hui outlines that consumption is 'something that happens in the course of doing something else' and that consumption practices require attention to relations (2012, p. 197). I am suggesting that tourists are preoccupied with 'doing something else' (Hui 2012, p. 197) when we are momentarily disoriented or distracted by environmental ideals or sensations; we are in the process

Figure 4.2 View from Reykjavík hostel window of snow-capped mountains (left); close up of the 'volcanic-looking' rocks in the footpath in downtown Reykjavík

of finding new relational groundings. This is a practice of consumption and production of experience, which leads to further potentials for future co-consumption of entangled experiences.

Re-orientations form into subtle yet affective (re)composures[1] with environments. New relationships are forged through environmental sensations and then, through collaborative compositions, new relations and sensations are produced, feeding out into the environmental entanglement. New pathways for collaborative practices are produced by bodily-environmental composures.

Two Environments: Nepal and Iceland

Nepal and Iceland are idealised destinations. They conjure many associations and expectations of what kinds of experiences are on offer to mediate tourist actions. Tourists to Nepal experience political instability, earthquakes, long-term power outages, and so on that make it 'difficult' to orient oneself. Travel to and around Iceland also presents challenges due to tumultuous weather patterns and seismic and volcanic activity. Despite these perceived 'risks', tourists are more influenced by idealised conceptions of each place as a unique experiential tourist destination (Frohlick 2003; Benediktsson, Lund and Huijbens 2011; Lund 2013; Pálsson 2013; Sverrisdóttir 2011). Although vastly different, both destinations overlap with this vivid imaginary in which tourists participate (Figures 4.3, 4.4, 4.5, and 4.6). What quickly emerged when I was observing and interviewing in these destinations was the influence that the environment has on tourists' preconceptions and, once they had arrived, how they negotiate these immense physical and psychological geographies. By positioning my own experiences in Iceland and Nepal as the driving point for analysis, the photographs and extracts of my fieldwork journal are the data that merges ethnographic fieldwork and first-person experience to provide reflection on moments of re-orientation with the environment.

Preconceived notions of a destination fit within a cultural imaginary comprised of social, environmental, and spatio-geographical influences to be consumed and experienced (for instance, see Karen Oslund's discussions of idealisations of the Icelandic 'North', 2005; and Katrín Lund's 2013 extension of Oslund). Tourists' imaginings of each destination frequently mismatches their experiences, and alongside the promises of tourist marketing, it does not account for the challenges and at times restrictive travel paths of a given destination. Yet, more importantly, a destination is not 'bound to specific environments or place images' (Bærenholdt, Haldrup, Larsen and Urry 2004, p. 2). Instead, they are formed through 'the corporeal and social *performances* of tourists', where 'the human body *engages* with the

Figure 4.3 Streets of Thamel, the tourist district in Kathmandu, Nepal (left); prayer flags wrapped around electrical wires on the side of the building in Kathmandu (right)

Figure 4.4 Sunrise over Pokhara, Nepal

natural world and hence produces spaces and places, rather than simply being located within them, or having them inscribed on its surface' (2004, p. 2, original emphasis). Preconceived and imaginary notions contrast with actual experiences when on-the-ground. This implies that destinations are

Figure 4.5 Photograph taken on the main ring road that circles Iceland. Postcard imagery at every bend in the road

Figure 4.6 Winter sunrise at 10:02am in the small town of Dalvík, Northern Iceland

constantly re-configuring through the action of persons who are being affected in turn by the environment. Collaboration, in this sense, reshapes and re-composes the relations between tourists and environments.

The moment in which ideals confront or conflict with experiences and sensations needs to be examined. The negation of spatial and geographical concerns in particular account for a great degree of disconnect or mismatching of expectation and experience. At the point of entry to each destination the generic re-orientations of jetlag and time zone differences and seasons present themselves to tourists. In my own experiences, the process of re-orientation often demands attention to heightened sensory awareness, the differences in aesthetics and cultural interactions, and the embodied process of situating oneself within immersive environments such as mountain ranges, glaciers, and other 'extreme' natural phenomenon (Barry 2017). Actions that tourists undertake provide examples where expectations of the destination are contrasted against lived experiences that are equally immersive and disorienting; even the everyday or mundane actions might be magnified by the new and unfamiliar conditions. To set oneself up to be receptive to the point at which ideals confront sensations, there needs to be a consideration of one's embedded perspectives. As a researcher and a tourist, I began to notice that an emphasis on bodily-environmental awareness opens the possibility of collaborative engagements. In such an approach, the everyday experiences cannot be separated out as individual ideals or desires. Therefore, moments of collective mobilities that switch between self-reflexive and collaborative need to be considered.

To illustrate these experiences, I draw from my fieldwork notes and photographic documentation, taken from the perspective of a researcher-tourist. Examining fieldwork experiences as co-productive values the process-based and situated perspectives that are driven by 'spaces of encounter and experience' (Scarles 2010, p. 906). Caroline Scarles describes being a 'researcher-as-tourist' in which she shared the 'anticipation of place' while engaging in touristic activities (2010, p. 914). This blended role, of being witness to action but being an actor bound by the environmental intensities, is a task that responds to the interconnection of multi-sensory encounters that question the role of individualised subjectivity in research (Pink 2009). This involves recognition that the researcher cannot be simply an observer, as they are always embedded in the situation. It also demonstrates the fusion of *all* actors in any situation *as environment*. As I engage with the following excerpts from my fieldwork journal and photographs, my actions are intrinsically linked to, and informed by, my reflections as a researcher. The first example in Nepal emphasises the materiality of tourist-environment relationships. The second example in Iceland hones in on how environmental intensities affect and alter the packing process. I use these insights to offer a multi-fragmented recollection that emphasises the experiences that exceed my expected tourist actions in favour of collaborative engagements with environments.

Moving With/in Nepal

Like many tourists, I approached my trip to Nepal with idealised notions of Himalayan vistas, made available to me by simply being in Nepal. Upon arrival, it quickly became evident to me that unless out on a trekking route, pristine views of these giant mountains are relatively scarce from the cities.

When I did see my first glimpse of a Himalayan peak, I was overjoyed at the scale of the mountains and the way they dominate the sky above. However, when gazing at the peak from a rooftop café in Pokhara, although it was picturesque, I would hardly describe it as an immersive experience of the environment. Instead, such experiences of (re)composure—due to environmental conditions—are often found in unexpected moments. When made aware of obscure and haptic interactions, when we move our bodies in unusual ways, when we collaboratively move with other tourists or objects, these are moments that reveal reconfigurations of body-environmental experiences.

For example, let me share an experience of a domestic flight within Nepal, between the cities of Pokhara and Kathmandu (Figure 4.7):

> The small twenty-seater plane climbed, breaching the clouds to reveal peaks glistening. Moving parallel to the Himalaya, the view was fragmented by the nine small cabin windows on the left side of the plane. People clamber around the cabin, despite the seatbelt sign being on. Climbing over each other, strangers holding each other's cameras, taking photos for each other. Sitting on each other, sharing the access to the windows. While we flew, little attention was paid to the flashing warning lights and alarms from the cockpit, as the plane bumped around in turbulence. The weight of shifting bodies tilted the plane, as

Figure 4.7 The Himalayan range seen on the flight from Pokhara to Kathmandu

the flight attendant tried in vain to get everyone to remain seated. Our experience was distant, yet we were captivated by the Himalaya.

(Journal extract, 30 September 2013)

On the surface, this event could be a purely visual engagement or a visual consumption of a landscape. However, this experience was not a one-way tourist gaze, nor generic photography of landmarks. The actions reveal collaborative interactions of bodies and materials, prompted by the environment. The movements within the cabin and the fact that we were traversing the country in a plane made the linkages between visual and bodily sensations more evident as the proximities between people shifted. Although we were inside a pressurised aircraft cabin, flying probably a hundred kilometres away from the Himalayan range, this example demonstrates how environments have the ability to mediate tourist practices.

This flight route between the two Nepalese cities does not always afford vantage points of the Himalayas, and there are many 'joy flight' services offered to tourists in Nepal promising close encounters with Himalayan peaks. As far as I could tell, none of us in the plane had taken this flight expecting such clear, close views. It was merely quick transportation from one city to the other. What occurred was a breaching of personal boundaries (people sitting on each other, as strangers), a collective series of movements driven by the resonance of scale (of the Himalayan peaks in contrast to ourselves and the small aircraft) and the mesmerising qualities of the 'natural' aesthetics (the drifting clouds, the snow-capped peaks).

Perceptual (visual sensations) and conceptual (positions of scale and distance) movements occur in addition to the performative. The 'constantly shifting positions' (Benediktsson and Lund 2010, p. 8) of the environment—encompassing myself and fellow tourists, our positions and actions—mobilise the collective situation. It shifts from a static gaze that fixes the Himalayan landscape or something that is 'out there', to creating a situation l by the 'tension which distributes inside and outside, self and world' (Wylie in Merriman et al. 2008, p. 207). The actions in this situation became co-consumptive due to the collaborative experience. We were united with each other and the environment through unexpected and collaborative actions.

Moving With/in Iceland

In June when the daylight hours are long in Iceland, the experience of sunset united myself and other tourists with the environment (Figures 4.8 and 4.9):

I saw with two fellow tourists, who were also staying at the hostel, on the rocks in the West of Reykjavík, from about 10:30pm till after midnight.

Figure 4.8 Sunset in Reykjavík, June

Figure 4.9 The coloured light saturates the urban landscape

We were mesmerised by the sunset as it silhouetted Snæfellness in the distance. Immersed in the multi-coloured hue of the fading sunlight. Everything around us was bathed in a reddish-pinkish-orangey glow. The footpath, road, our bodies, all bathed. The sunset enveloped us.

(Journal extract, 5 June 2012)

But it was more than just light at high latitude; it was feeling the Nordic sunset, familiar to many, but ever so exotic and surreal for us as tourists only temporarily in the 'North'.

> Silence between us as we watched, waited, felt. After sunset we walked back to the hostel. It was after midnight, dark inside the dorm room. The 'dark' was a red-pink-orange, my vision was disoriented. I searched through my bag on the floor, fumbling for my pyjamas. I couldn't help but laugh about my vision, it felt like being mildly intoxicated and disoriented. On hearing my laughing, one of the guys I had been sitting with remarked that his vision was pink. Whispering, we all agreed. All we could see was the darkness, saturated with the pink that the sunset had impressed on our eyes. 'Now this is how you pack a bag in Iceland', he said to me. 'You have to go stare at the sunset for hours and then try to find your belongings in all the pink.'
>
> (Journal extract, 5 June 2012)

In an account that bears an uncanny resemblance to this experience, Erin Manning (2013) writes about the 'yellowness' of a kitchen wall illuminated by sunlight. She states, '[t]he luminosity is less object than field of relation. It is less color as such than compositional force' (2013, p. 25). Dis-orienting, situating, re-orienting. Manning describes this as 'an immediate feeling activated by the event of the light' (2013, p. 25). Manning's example and my recollection as a tourist are not mediations of experience through sunlight; it is one of the many ways in which we feel these environmental (re)composures that alter our actions and can attune us to how we are entangled with/in the environment. The light is not a simple overlay or connection to landscape and the room we were within, or a purely visual experience. Rather, it is part of the complex relationships formed between the objects, the architecture, the landscape, and us, which together constitute an environment.

Sensation, place, and practice shift, mingle, and merge to become part of the 'experiential complexity' of a 'comprehensive aesthetic' of the environment (Benediktsson 2007, p. 214). It is important to note that Karl Benediktsson is talking about landscapes and 'nature', yet I incorporate these as part of what constitutes the environment. I take his caution that a geography of such an environment needs to 'take visual values seriously' in order to delve into a realm of multi-sensory and aesthetic concerns (Benediktsson 2007, p. 214). More than a usual gaze, a tourist gaze, as John Urry and Jonas Larsen explain, is 'an embodied practice that involves senses beyond sight' (2011, p. 20). This embodied process draws on and extends idealisations and collective experiences of an environment, harnessing the actions occurring in the moment.

While we were awestruck by the saturation and intensity of the Nordic sunset, which hit the spot with the ideals of what the environment of Reykjavík might provide us as a touristic experience, it was the alteration to our everyday process of unpacking our bags and locating our pyjamas that resonated most strongly. Our vision blurred, saturated, and disorienting while we attempted to do such a mundane task shifted the environmental intensity directly to our bodies and the lived experience. No longer was the environment 'out there', separate to the human, but instead it was a part of us, embodied in our actions and prompting new collaborative re-orientations to our habits and practices.

What this tourism event makes evident is how individuality is breached through the relations between the destination, the season, and the bodies we felt through. The environment is manifested through the processes of re-orientation that are felt and consumed as movements across bodily-environmental composures. Individuals become disoriented and then, through a series of interactions with the environment, we re-orient and adjust, (re)composing and consuming the experiences that result. The heightened sensory awareness contrasts with daily routines, and at times it collides and alters our movements. When our attention is turned back to everyday practices, our positions have shifted and we feel these practices differently, attending to them in alternative ways. We have recalibrated ourselves and our sensations to be attuned to the environment we are with/in.

Moving with an environment is a collaborative experience that catalyses moments in tourism that make us aware of the ways in which we are moving and interacting with and in environments. In particular, this occurs through the felt-sensations of experience, the aesthetic intensities and movements that are required to carry out interactions with environmental conditions. The forms of collaboration that result allow us to share and relish co-consumptive experiences that are subtle movements and transitions.

Collaborative Re-orientation Experiences

The many subtle interactions and moments where actors are brought together in collaborative re-orientations reveal how tourist practices can transition through and with the environment. In each situation, the collaboration underpins our re-orientation with the environment. Although the first situation in Nepal does not involve packing, it does highlight a moment when environmental ideals and collective actions mediate and alter material and bodily thresholds. In the second situation, the intensity of the sunset triggered affects that resonated long after the touristic actions and infused into the mundane process of packing. Such actions overthrew the socio-cultural norms and the original expectations and ideals that fellow tourists and myself had of what experiences each destination would offer, and altered our routines and practices. I suggest that these environmental re-orientations offer new models of co-consumption and production of tourism mobilities. This is a tentative proposal that changes to a tourist's awareness of environmental conditions provide entry points for sustainable and alternative practices of tourism mobilities.

Collaborative actions are those that span a range of actors and pave new ways for interacting that frequently move across bodily thresholds. Composing with/in environments urges collective forms of movement. We move with other humans as well as environmental conditions in dynamic and spontaneous ways as we co-produce and co-consume experiences of mobilities. The composing forces of the environment might be found in obvious tourist examples, such as trekking through vast wilderness areas or taking a joy flight over a glacier. However, it can also be experienced in the more unconscious movements that our bodies carry out, such as in my experience of feeling the Nordic sunset that saturated my vision and altered my ability to carry out the task of searching through my bag. These subtle or more mundane instances where we re-orient with environments alter our mobile experiences and force us to adapt our practices. Moments when we are moving and in transition with the environment provide opportunities for reflection on our practices that are simultaneously subtle yet immersive, co-consumptive, and productive.

For instance, Tim Ingold (2010) eloquently draws our attention to how the action of breathing encompasses our bodies and environments in a complex entanglement. We are 'at once a body-on-the-ground and a body-in-the-air. Earth and sky, then, are not components of an external environment . . . They are rather regions of the body's very existence' (Ingold 2010, p. 116). Breathing, as well as many other experiences specific to tourism or encountered in our daily movements, marks an interdependence of our bodies with the environment (Braidotti 2008, p. 182) in moments where individual experiences shift towards collective immersions across human and nonhuman actors. This could be gazing at the sunset or taking photographs of the Himalaya. These actions point towards moments where our experiences are beyond human actions, where the environment primes us for certain kinds of experiences and awareness.

Awareness is the critical factor for focusing and emphasising how 'everyday' tourist actions facilitate practices of (re)composing with environmental conditions. Possibilities arise that can induce changes to tourists' attitudes and behaviours, where an immersive environmental experience becomes achievable to consume without undertaking more extreme (often high-impact) outdoor activities.

Having a greater awareness of collaborative experiences gives a subtler, affirmative, and, more importantly, an achievable awareness of the potential experiences that we, as tourists, can have. To stress the subtleties of my examples, I want to emphasise that individualised consumption is overturned in favour of haptic awareness and collaborative approaches. Acknowledging that we are part of the environment and that it alters our bodily sensations and influences our actions shifts collaboration beyond the human scale. This is a new form of co-consumption and practice that is collective and entangled with an array of actors. This combination opens possible reconfiguring of the existing relationships, or towards re-orientation and openness to unfamiliar relationships for which there is no prior experience. In this light, the type of activity that gives rise to experience is less important than the mode of engagement and attention to the collective re-orientations with the environment. Therefore, to some extent the less impactful experiences offer more opportunity for experiencing and consuming specific environments, since these activities are less populated by idealised and preconceived notions of meaning and value.

If we, as tourists and in our everyday movements, could harness environmental experiences and value them as important encounters with/in each destination, then surely types of tourism behaviour and activities could perhaps be less impactful, dramatic, or dominating. Although this might seem idealistic, I feel that my own examples of re-orienting environmental experiences were far more enriching acquisitions of tourism mobilities than the pre-packaged marketing to individuals of a destination that waits ready for me to consume. What this means for practices of mobilities—whether at home on our daily commute, or afar in some unfamiliar landscape—is that the 'everyday' presents a turbulent and lively set of potential encounters that can inspire us, ignite our imaginations, and go beyond touristic ideals and expectations. Such minute or subtle instances where our actions are altered and we re-orient unsettle our senses as we reposition ourselves in new, collaborative, and enriching situations.

What can be gleaned from tourism scenarios is that by positioning and acknowledging ourselves as not only tourists, but in a constant state of transiting and being mobile in a range of situations, the conditions are set up for transformation and collective experiences. If we are able to position ourselves as always mobile and open to a constant state of adjustment with the environmental conditions, we can use this state to induce more collaborative relationships in tourism activities. This would imply turning away from actions oriented to individual consumption and moving towards an enhanced multi-sensory engagement where we co-consume experiences that are collaboratively produced with environments. For example, subtle, everyday practices could be favoured over high-impact activities where the experience is constructed for an individual, which at times has a detrimental impact on environmental qualities. The expectation for what tourists can consume are therefore more sustainable, in the sense that they can be more immersive, more multi-sensual, resulting in a collaborative, situated experience of mobilities and travel.

The manner in which consumptive actions are bound to practices (Warde 2005, pp. 146–147) requires attention to both the obvious practices of consumption in tourism (for instance, purchasing souvenirs or participating in tours) and the idealised cultural experiences that tourists seek to acquire. The mixing of both individualised consumption behaviours in tourism and the broader collective idealisations that tourism cultures in certain destinations propound, complement, and reinforce the urgency for an awareness of the under-examined subtleties that are occurring in tourism actions. How these tourist practices inform our everyday practices, whether we are travelling away from or in our local environments, influences the broader sets of mobile practices that we engage in, too.

Sustainability, in this sense, could be tourists beginning to feel these moments of re-orientation as a collaborative (re)composition of and with the environment. When tourists begin to feel these moments, these subtle collaborative actions that actualise bodily-environmental movements, perhaps these moments of realisation, these felt movements, could elicit an understanding of tourism practices and appreciation of destinations that can be collectively negotiated. This is consistent with Thrift's observations that

> it has become clear that these flows of subjectivity need to and do involve more actors—various kinds of things, various other biological beings, even the heft of a particular landscape—in a continuous undertow of matterings that cannot be reduced to simple transactions but can become part of new capacities to empower.
>
> (Thrift 2007, p. viii)

By reconsidering the boundaries between subjects and objects as an intermeshing of human and nonhuman actions, this also 'shifts in what is understood as "environment"' (Thrift 2007, p. 97). What was once an abstracted, empty void, somehow conjured through ideals of the external or the 'natural', is liberated through collaborative approaches.

From Collaborative Re-orientations to Alternative Mobile Practices

There are many experiences in tourism that highlight the interdependence of our actions with/in a specific environment. The examples I have detailed here are a selection of moments during tourism in which sensations and movements congeal to afford new experiences and understandings of environments. Becoming aware of these processes allows minute and subtle shifts in our practices to emerge during moments of transition and mobility. Moments when we do not resist collective movements open the possibility of enactive relationships in which we are composed by and are composing with environments. It is within such moments that an alert and ecologically concerned practice of tourism mobilities can begin to develop and new forms of co-consumption can produce enriching experiences.

There is an imperative that we take heed of our actions when we are moving, becoming aware of the more subtle, less-impactful movements that can be carried out while still maintaining a heightened touristic experience. In doing so, techniques that move beyond individualised consumptive patterns towards collective and collaborative co-consumption and production are foregrounded. This may occur as a re-evaluation of what it means to consume a landscape or destination, or explore ways in which the scales of movements erode both the cultural imaginary and the ability of the land to maintain the very eco-system that draws tourists in.

In the examples I have given from my own tourist experiences with/in Nepal and Iceland, I have detailed a proposition for new awareness to collaborative practices of tourism mobilities. These are moments that transcend the human–nonhuman division, if only momentarily. When a sunset bleeds into our vision, disorienting our habitual sensations and expectations for what action we intend to undertake, a movement that is beyond the individual human emerges. My individualised ideals of what I expected to experience and consume shifted and made way for unexpected, yet still immersive, environmental (re)composures. Such experiences 'continue to saturate our activities afterwards' (Barry 2017, p. 12) and 'prompt us to reposition ourselves not as the singular, unifying force, but instead as being composed through relations with the many other actors that we are moving with' (p. 11). They reveal the extent that the environment influences our perceptions and how a heightened sensory awareness induced by environmental conditions contrasts with our everyday routines. It is a congealing of bodily-environmental movements that we adapt into new practices. When we later turn our attention back to the more mundane, routine, or habitual actions, we have (re) composed with the environment and new relationships have been forged that are beyond our individualised expectations and actions.

Understanding the environment as an actor that tourists move with/in makes it possible to reconsider the environment's role in the formation of mobile experiences. The implications are that actions across all actors— human and nonhuman—and across all scales—from traversing an unknown landscape to the minute and mundane process of packing—are altered and influenced by movements that are beyond our individual intentions and lead to collaborative mobile practices. Through such experiences it becomes possible to alter and offer new approaches to tourism and a broad set of mobile situations that target the foundations between idealised imaginings and actual lived experiences as we move with environments.

Note

1 I use the term '(re)composure' to signal the ongoing formation and assemblage of actors with/in the environment. This draws from the definitions of 'composure' from Latour (2010) and Deleuze and Guattari (2004). See Chapter 1 for my exploration of the term 'composition' and the relationship to communal practices.

References

Alaimo, S. 2008. 'Trans-corporeal feminisms and the ethical space of nature'. *In*: Alaimo, S. and Heckman, S. eds. *Material feminisms*. Bloomington and Indianapolis: Indiana University Press, pp. 237–264.

Anderson, J. 2013. 'Exploring the consequences of mobility: Reclaiming jet lag as the state of travel disorientation', *Mobilities*, vol. 10, no. 1, pp. 1–16. doi:10.108 0/17450101.2013.806392

Bærenholdt, J.O., Haldrup, M., Larsen, J. and Urry, J. 2004. *Performing tourist places*. Aldershot and Burlington: Ashgate.

Barad, K. 2007. *Meeting the universe half way: Quantum physics and the entanglement of matter and meaning*. Durham and London: Duke University Press.

Barry, K. 2017. 'Transversal travels: The relational movements and environmental intensities of packing a bag', *Studies in Material Thinking*, vol. 16, pp. 1–17.

Barry, K. and Keane, J. 2017. 'Moving within mobilities: Expanding spatial experiences through the artwork PAN & ZOOM', *Applied Mobilities*, vol. 2, no. 1, pp. 67–84. doi:10.1080/23800127.2016.1272971

Bech, H., Borch, C. and Larsen, S.N. 2010. 'Resistance, politics, space, architecture: Interview with Nigel Thrift', *Distinktion: Scandinavian Journal of Social Theory*, vol. 11, no. 2, pp. 93–105.

Benediktsson, K. 2007. '"Scenophobia", geography and the aesthetic politics of landscape', *Geografiska Annaler*, vol. 89, no. 3, pp. 203–217. doi:10.1111/j.1468-0467.2007.00249.x

Benediktsson, K. and Lund, K.A. eds. 2010. 'Introduction: Starting a conversation with landscape'. *In*: *Conversations with landscape*. Farnham: Ashgate, pp. 1–12.

Benediktsson, K., Lund, K.A. and Huijbens, E. 2011. 'Inspired by eruptions? Eyjafjallajökull and Icelandic tourism', *Mobilities*, vol. 6, no. 1, pp. 77–84. doi:10.1080/17450101.2011.532654

Bennett, J. 2010. *Vibrant matter: A political ecology of things*. Durham: Duke University Press.

Braidotti, R. 2008. 'The politics of life as Bios/Zoe'. *In*: A. Smelik and N. Lykke, eds. *Bits of life: Feminism at the intersections of media, bioscience, and technology*. Seattle: University of Washington Press, pp. 177–192.

Braidotti, R. 2012. *Nomadic theory: The portable Rosi Braidotti*. New York: Columbia University Press.

Bryant, L. 2011. *The democracy of objects.* Open Humanities Press. Retrieved 26 August 2016, from: http://hdl.handle.net/2027/spo.9750134.0001.001

Deleuze, G. and Guattari, F. 2004. *A thousand plateaus: Capitalism and schizophrenia,* trans. B. Massumi. London: Continuum.

Frohlick, S.E. 2003. 'Negotiating the 'global' within the global playscapes of Mount Everest', *Canadian Review of Sociology and Anthropology,* vol. 40, no. 5, pp. 525–542.

Gendlin, E. 2013. 'Arakawa and Gins: The organism-person-environment process', *Inflexions,* vol. 6, pp. 222–233. Retrieved 3 August 2016 from www.inflexions. org/n6_gendlin.pdf

Gins, M. and Arakawa, S. 2002. *Architectural body.* Tuscaloosa: University of Alabama Press.

Hui, A. 2012. 'Things in motion, things in practices: How mobile practice networks facilitate the travel and use of leisure objects', *Journal of Consumer Culture,* vol. 12, no. 2, pp. 195–215. doi:10.1177/1469540512446873

Huijbens, E. and Benediktsson, K. 2013. 'Inspiring the visitor? Landscapes and horizons of hospitality', *Tourist Studies,* vol. 13, no. 2, pp. 189–208. doi:10.1177/146879613490378

Ingold, T. 2010. 'Footprints through the weather-world: Walking, breathing, knowing'. *In:* T. Marchland, ed. *Making knowledge: Explorations of the indissoluble relation between mind, body, and environment.* Oxford: Wiley-Blackwell, pp. 115–132.

Latour, B. 2007. *Reassembling the social.* New York: Oxford University Press.

Latour, B. 2010. 'An attempt at a "compositionist manifesto"', *New Literary History,* vol. 41, no. 3, pp. 471–490.

Law, J. and Singleton, V. 2013. 'ANT and politics: Working in and on the world', *Qualitative Sociology,* vol. 36, no. 4, pp. 485–502. doi:10.1007/s11133-013-9263-7

Lien, M.E. and Law, J. 2011. '"Emergent Aliens": On salmon, nature, and their enactment', *Ethnos: Journal of Anthropology,* vol. 76, no. 1, pp. 65–87. doi:10.1080/00141844.2010.549946

Lim, F.K.G. 2008. 'Of reverie and emplacement: Spatial imaginings and tourism encounters in Nepal Himalaya', *Inter-Asia Cultural Studies,* vol. 9, no. 3, pp. 375–394. doi:10.1080/14649370802184452

Lund, K.A. 2013. 'Experiencing nature in nature-based tourism', *Tourist Studies,* vol. 13, no. 2, pp. 156–171. doi:10.1177/1468797613490373

Manning, E. 2013. *Always more than one.* Durham, NC: Duke University Press.

Massey, D. 2006. 'Landscape as provocation: Reflections on moving mountains', *Journal of Material Culture,* vol. 11, nos. 1/2, pp. 33–48. doi:10.1177/1359183506062991

Merriman, P., Revill, G., Cresswell, T., Lorimer, H., Matless, D., Rose, G. and Wylie, J. 2008. 'Landscape, mobility, practice', *Social & Cultural Geography,* vol. 9, no. 2, pp. 191–212. doi:10.1080/14649360701856136

Morton, T. 2007. *Ecology without nature: Rethinking environmental aesthetics.* Cambridge, MA and London: Harvard University Press.

Oslund, K. 2005. '"The North begins inside": Imagining Iceland as wilderness and homeland', *GHI Bulletin,* vol. 36, Spring, pp. 91–99.

Pálsson, G. 2013. 'Ensembles of biosocial relations'. *In*: T. Ingold and G. Palsson, eds. *Biosocial becomings: Integrating social and biological anthropology.* New York: Cambridge University Press, pp. 22–41.

Pink, S. 2009. *Doing sensory ethnography.* London: Sage.

Ren, C. Jóhannesson, G.T. and Van der Duim, R. 2012. 'How ANT works'. *In*: R. Van der Duim, C. Ren and G.T. Jóhannesson, eds. *Actor-network theory and tourism: Ordering, materiality and multiplicity.* Oxon: Routledge, pp. 13–25.

Scarles, C. 2010. 'Where words fail, visual ignite: Opportunities for visual autho-ethnography in tourism research', *Annals of Tourism Research*, vol. 37, no. 4, pp. 905–926. doi:10.1016/j.annals.2010.02.001

Sverrisdóttir, H. 2011. 'The destination within', *Journal of the Association of Icelandic Geographers/Landabréfið*, vol. 25, pp. 77–84.

Thrift, N. 2006. 'Space', *Theory Culture Society*, vol. 23, no. 2–3, pp. 139–146. doi:10.1177/0263276406063780

Thrift, N. 2007. *Non-representational theory: Space, politics, affect.* London: Routledge.

Urry, J. and Larsen, J. 2011. *The tourist gaze 3.0.* London: SAGE Publication Ltd.

Van der Duim, R., Ren, C. and Jóhannesson, G.T. 2012. *Actor-network theory and tourism: Ordering, materiality and multiplicity.* London and New York: Routledge.

Warde, A. 2005. 'Consumption and theories of practice', *Journal of Consumer Culture*, vol. 5, no. 2, pp. 131–153. doi:10.1177/1469540505053090

Waterhouse, J., Reilly, T., Atkinson, G. and Edwards, B. 2007. 'Jet lag: Trends and coping strategies', *Lancet*, March 31–April 6, pp. 1117–1129.

5 Practices for Future Transitions

Throughout this book I have advocated that everyday practices developed during travel—the small, mundane, or routine procedures—are important in harnessing alternative experiences and expectations of mobility. Everyday practices can, and do, influence how tourists consider their consumption and experiences and can be used to intensify the consideration of what constitutes sustainable forms of tourism mobilities. Although my focus is on tourism, which is just one of the many forms of interrelated mobilities that are growing in global society (Gren and Huijbens 2014; Urry 2016; Urry and Larsen 2011), the practices that tourism deploys can easily be applied to daily life. Tourism experiences are the result of both local and global interactions that draw attention to the multi-sensual relationships that each movement instigates. My interest lies in how we *practice* mobilities in our everyday encounters, and how this connects to touristic ideals yet prompts new modalities and collective experiences.

Valuing everyday practices as creative and collective forms of knowledge production cultivates a more inclusive and sustainable understanding of movement. One of the key factors to understanding the implications of the shifts from individual to collective forms of movement experiences is the sensitivity to how we are situated within macro and micro scales of movement. These moments expose our capacity to alter and attune to being in transition and how individual boundaries become increasingly fluid depending on who (and what) we encounter and travel with and which pathways we decide to follow. In turn, these practices feed back into future movements and compositions, creating situated, affective, and collective experiences of mobility.

I began this book with my experience at the base of Eyjafjallajökull, the small erupting Icelandic volcano whose ash had infused my clothes, shoes, backpack, and future travels. It was also an event that temporarily halted international aviation and threw global flows into disarray by drawing attention to the environmental and material agencies that support, restrict, or enable human mobility. This moment fuelled my inquiry into the agency of nonhumans and the practices that tourists develop, share, and adapt. Throughout the subsequent discussions, I have used packing to advocate for increased attention to human–nonhuman interactions that are formed through mobilities and result in collaborative co-consumption practices. Packing and many other mundane, routine practices that tourists undertake are indicative of relationships and encounters with a variety of nonhumans (both material and immaterial). During packing, moments when we interact with materials often require a slight shift in habitual processes to form new adaptive movements as we negotiate the task at hand. Encounters with materials also encompass complex spatialities that inflect various sociocultural and idealised notions of travel techniques and the manoeuvres that are required of tourists. In particular, the communal spaces within hostelling accommodation are conducive of collective forms of movement and draw attention to the many scales that human and nonhuman action operate within. Being aware of how tourists inflect and interact with each other, with their belongings, or the communal atmospheres and environmental conditions often necessitates individual actions to be repositioned in favour of collective forms of consumption and co-productive experiences. The practice of packing has been central to an increase in one's attunement to the way that we construct relationships as we move. It is emblematic of a practice of mobilities that connects tourists to both global concerns and everyday actions. In this final chapter, I reflect upon the two main themes of the book—*collective interactions* and *globalised mobilities*—to explore the meanings we instil into the process of packing, the practices that are generated, and the potential for new, creative, and collaborative modes of knowledge.

How We Transited to Here

It is clear that large-scale movements of people around the Earth are on the rise, and there are no indications of slowing. More people are on the move than ever before, with over 1 billion international journeys taken each year (UNWTO 2016) and an estimated 16 million refugees in the world (UNHCR 2015). Just these two figures alone indicate how individual actions are necessarily influenced and dictated by global mobility flows. And these figures only focus on human travellers, not taking into account the thousands of shipping containers, consumer products, minerals, waste, bacteria, and other nonhumans that are moved around the Earth with and for humans (Bennett 2010; Clark and Hird 2014; Haldrup and Larsen 2010; Urry 2014; Van der Duim, Ren and Jóhannesson 2012). Each movement pushes, pulls, and stretches us in various ways, and we develop practices to adapt and transform ourselves to fit within the uncertainties of where we are going or the imaginative desires and ideals of what we will experience next. I am suggesting that *practicing mobilities* involves negotiating the complexity of individual movements that fit within larger systems and navigating the relationships that are forged through movement.

The challenge, then, is how to untangle the interconnected movements and extract the practices that individuals develop to aid in situating themselves and understanding movement. This involves being able to identify how individual practices inflect and are informed by larger global scales and trends. In the following two sections, I elaborate on how the two themes that run through this book—collective interactions and global mobilities—influence the practices that are generated as we move. Together, the themes indicate how practices of tourism mobilities, particularly within the example of packing, are shaped by and contribute to alternative, creative, and collaborative knowledges.

Collective Interactions

Practicing mobility involves adapting, creating, and collaborating as we adjust ourselves to fit within the flux of movements. As I have shown, the process of packing a bag is a practice that involves sensing and executing movement across various scales and sensations, which draws us into an entanglement of actors that influence our movements. This can be in the slightest of sensations, at the peripheries of our experiences, such as the minute shifts of materials when we are pushing and shoving clothes into an overflowing suitcase (see Chapter 2). Or it could be in awe-inspiring experiences when we witness vast, immense landscapes that disorient us (see Chapter 4). In addition, these shifts across scales—from macro to micro, individual and collective—signal that there are many kinds of movement experiences that take place on a range of sensory registers. To *practice* being mobile implies an attention to the relation of actors that we are moving with, and the way that our movements operate 'within and across' different 'registers of activity' (Barry and Keane 2017, p. 69). Part of the challenge is finding opportunities that expand on how we come to know and experience mobility, which might operate across corporeal, imaginative, objective, virtual, or communicative registers (Urry 2011, pp. 24–25). It requires honing in on moments when we become aware of the collective movements of which we are a part.

There is caution, though. It is important not to over-animate every situation, actor, or movement. While it is easy to claim that everything is in motion and that movement prevails, and we should be open and adaptable to transitions, awareness of the 'differentiated movements' (Merriman

2016, p. 559) that distribute agency across materials and actions is required. There must be sensitivity to the 'social, cultural, political and economic geographies of different senses of movement and stillness' (Merriman 2016, p. 559). Not everyone or everything has the capacity to move or the desire to be on the move. Many movements rely on stillness, restriction, and inequality (Bissel and Fuller 2011; Merriman 2016; Urry 2016). Mobilities are not all equal, nor do all actors have agency or exercise their agency on an even playing field. Instead, an affirmative approach to difference is needed, in order to better understand the capacities and impacts of movements and what 'binds us together' (Braidotti 2016). This is particularly applicable to tourism mobilities, where an individual's desires and consumption behaviours are not always considered as having an effect or impact on anyone but the individual tourist. In order to evaluate the practices that permit movement or compensate for unexpected movements, recognition is warranted for the connections across various modes of movement that might usually be taken for granted. Sensitivity to micro movements, such as minute, banal, or everyday routines, is manageable for most tourists. When one attunes to such moments, there is a conceptual shift that occurs within the movement of one set of relation to another. That is, an individual repositions themselves in relation to the world, and their understanding of the world is equally moved in relation to this new attunement. Movements that are imaginary, projective, or empathetic help to visualise and understand how, where, and what we are moving with. Awareness can be cultivated through the mutually constructed movements in which we consider ourselves beyond the immediacy of our own experience and open to the spatiotemporal shifts as they unfold (see Chapter 3). *Collective interactions*, in this sense, bring to focus the myriad of mobilities that we are bound with/in.

Examining the procedures that can be developed during travel involves reflecting on how we are 'in the act' (Lorimer in Merriman et al. 2008, p. 196) and responsive to our surroundings. I have used the investigation into packing as an entry point to the practices that tourists use to situate themselves and adjust to a variety of other actors and influences. However, tourist practices are not always routinised or ready-made techniques that fit every situation. There is no instruction manual that codifies experiences or shows us how to practice being a tourist (Barry 2015). Instead, we are left with 'messy relations' (Ren, Jóhannesson and Van der Duim 2012, p. 14; Veijola, Molz, Pyyhtinen, Höckert and Grit 2014) that we fumble, stumble, and stagger through as we try to sort our belongings and find some sense of orientation. Timothy Cresswell posits that too often practice is considered as 'being about exceptional and rarefied moments' (in Merriman et al. 2008, p. 195). Perhaps understanding practice is more about following 'the flows of people and things' in order to 'gain a *sense* of it' (Pink 2012, p. 33, original emphasis). Examining practices in this vein relies on movement and the relationships forged through movement. It involves considering how objects and materials—nonhumans—frequently alter our intentions and actions or 'force us to think differently' (Bissell 2009, p. 96). Allison Hui (2013) proposes thinking of practice and mobility as intertwined, so that practices are not isolated from the final event, but rather an ongoing process or set of interactions. She argues that it 'provides a way of recognizing the importance of not only people's movement but also the interdependent and heterogeneous mobilities of elements that structure and sustain established social practices' (2013, p. 892). Packing, and many other everyday practices, urges us to think and practice movement across different speeds and registers, in moments when nonhumans choreograph and alter our intended actions (Manning 2013, pp. 92–93; see Chapter 3), or when movements are 'both prompted and experienced by the object' (Bissell 2009, p. 96). These are moments when we might begin to think 'processually' (Manning 2013, p. 32) and conceive of our individual actions as bound within collective movements. When this type of awareness is cultivated, the need for alternative practices of mobilities that value creative and communal actions begin to take shape.

The feeling of being in a *collective* of human–nonhuman action might not be at the forefront of our thoughts, especially when we are in the midst of a mundane task or routine. However, tourism mobilities frequently offer situations where we experience being part of the global flows (Mol and Law 1994; Urry 2003). By 'collective', I do not meet a homogenous overarching concept for working through global issues or tourism as a whole. Instead, following Bruno Latour, I use the word collective as 'precisely the *work* of collecting into a whole' (2004, p. 59, original emphasis), where the prominence is on the process and not the final collective form as a fixed or static position. Latour reminds us that 'If we use the word "collective" in the singular, it is thus not in order to signal the same type of unity as the one implied by the term "nature" ' (2004, p. 59). Collective interactions, therefore, are heterogeneous and are constantly altering, reconfiguring, and reassembling in new moments of action. The practices in tourism that enable us to collect ourselves, such as gathering together our belongings, sorting through clothes, or discarding used tickets and receipts, are moments that subtly draw attention to how our experiences are assemblages of individual human intentions and an array of nonhumans that support, enable, or disrupt, unravel, or re-route our actions.

Globalised Mobilities

There is urgency that we reconsider the scale and impact of tourism mobilities. The Anthropocene—the current geological era that recognises the extent to which human action has altered the Earth's systems (Gren and Huijbens 2014; Palsson et al. 2013; Latour 2014)—has initiated drastic shifts in the perception of human movements. Increasing international tourism (particularly via aeromobilities) plays a significant role in the movement of people and materials around the Earth, and as Martin Gren and Edward Huijbens suggest, tourism is now on the scale of a 'geological force' (2014). The Anthropocene presents us with a complexity that requires us to think and act in alternative measures, taking into consideration human action within a realm of nonhuman and Earthly scales. Timothy Morton describes the Anthropocene as a particularly 'strange' concept to grasp (2013, p. 20), much like climate change, because it operates on 'profoundly different temporalities than the human-scale ones we are used to' (p. 1). In addition, the places that we visit are often presented as unique destinations, but where 'the Earth is quite absent' (Gren and Huijbens 2012, p. 160) because tourists are fixated on a particular point that they travel to. In some environmental tourist destinations, our position and location on the Earth is momentarily disrupted by the large scales of geological features or the 'Earthly' residues that we come into contact with in certain places (see Chapter 4). However, there is an ongoing mis-matching of preconceived tourist ideals, experience, and geographical reference of how our movements are positioned on a global scale. Due to these abstracted and multi-scalar representations of the 'global', it can be challenging to conceive of what kind of impact an individual tourist's actions have on the global mobility stage.

The concerns that the Anthropocene brings to the foreground, particularly anthropogenic climate change, sits in contrast to the (Western) ideals of nomadism that propel tourism. With increasing global tourism, there is a perpetuation of tourist imagery, destination marketing, and ideals of the ease and luxury of travel that is open to everyone. The reality is that only those with the 'right' passport and wealth have safe access to travel, and to the opportunity of being a 'global nomad' (Richards and Wilson 2004). John Urry offers a crucial insight that '[t]here is an ideology of movement' (2016, p. 18). Those with the right to move can select what kinds of movements they undertake, for how long, and what objects they can move with. It is precisely this delicate balance of freedom and constraint that the materiality of what we travel with (packed in our bags) brings into focus.

While there are immense differences between people who are travelling for leisure and those who are seeking refuge or are forcibly on the move, there are some commonalities of experience and concerns of how everyone moves in global society. Whether this is in the types of objects that we move with, the consumption and discarding of objects (such as one-use-only plastic travel sized toiletries), or the amount of things that we can physically carry with us, the agency of materials brings to the foreground common concerns. For example, the photographic project 'What's in my bag?' by Tyler Jump and the International Refugee Committee (2015) is a prime example of how packing a bag and material agencies intersect with global mobility concerns. The photographs depict Syrian refugees (adults, children, and families) and their remaining possessions laid out on the ground: small assortments of medication, toiletries, family jewellery, and smartphones, unpacked from old, dirty, or torn backpacks and handbags. While this photographic project gained international media attention, it sparked criticism about the belongings (particularly smartphones and sim cards) and whether the monetary value of an item should strip their legitimacy of being a refugee (see Channel 4 News 2016; Ram 2015). It is unfathomable that these material belongings held such power when unpacked for the world to witness, but it raises urgent questions about the agency and potency of the global relationships and ideals that form through materials and movements.

The increasing circulation of people and materials around the world necessitates new ways to negotiate and interrogate the encounters we have with mobile subjects (both human and nonhuman). This might start at the micro, individual level, of considering how much 'stuff' we consume and thinking about the material constitution of our consumption patterns. Or it might be to re-evaluate the desires to travel to certain destinations and how these are informed by marketing and tourism cultures. After all, tourism relies on relationships that are formed through 'the placing of people, materials, images and the systems of difference and similarity that they perform' (Haldrup and Larsen 2010, p. 65). Tourists might re-evaluate what constitutes a 'good' tourism experience, or how interest can be found by attending to the more mundane and routine actions, or the haphazard moments that take us by surprise and unsettle our intentions in unexpected ways (see Chapters 3 and 4). Valuing alternative modes of experience requires a change and 'calls for recompositions of both subjectivity and community' (Braidotti 2013, p. 83).

As materials (such as resources and minerals, and arguably passports and visas) become more prominent in global debates of how the world moves, then the agency of materials is key in how we connect to the many international, ethical, socio-cultural, and environmental transitions ahead. It is too simplistic to suggest that international travel for tourism and leisure purposes should be halted to slow the effects of carbon emissions. However, to some degree tourists can become more aware and informed of the relationships of their movements to global systems. I am suggesting that one way to negotiate and understand these encounters is to add emphasis to more subtle, mundane, or smaller-scale practices. The everyday practices that tourists do, such as packing, can become significant in understanding our position in global flows. Alternative modes of experiences and desires are needed for tourists to help situate themselves within these flows and conceive of their actions in different ways.

Propositions for Sustainable Tourist Practices

Finding new ways to practice tourism mobilities requires attention to the collective moments when we are open to alternative modes of inhabiting and participating. When packing does not go to plan, when clothes topple out from an overflowing bag, or when the communal space of a hostel dormitory requires adjustment of individual habits, these are movements when tourists are moving towards a processual subjectivity that is responsive to material, spatial, and environmental interactions. Such moments encourage tourists to consider the impact, consumption, and ideals of everyday practices.

For many of the tourists I spoke with, and in my own personal experience of packing every day in hostels for months on end, packing becomes 'the everyday'. One tourist explained to me that packing was his everyday routine, where he was packing so often that 'you try and find structure within it, you create structure in it'. He suggested that 'it's quite therapeutic. The packing, washing dishes, doing those sorts of routine chores, kind of opens your mind, you allow yourself just to drift while you do it'. Another tourist reflected on their packing practices, stating, 'I think that's part of what I enjoy about camping and travelling is . . . that idea of everything I need is in that bag'. These comments demonstrate that although packing is a mundane, everyday routine, for many tourists it is a practice that assembles meaning and purpose for their day and to aid their travel. Another tourist described the relationship she felt to her bag and belongings: 'It is because you have less objects, and you somehow create a certain relationship to, or I mean, it gets a bigger value, the small things, that normally back home would be nothing'. It is in these moments, when we feel the intensity of the process, and become aware of our relationships to things around us, that everyday tourist practices become more than simply manoeuvring ourselves and our belongings. At the point where experiences, sensations, and ideals merge, new practices and meanings emerge.

For some tourists, packing is a practice that develops into a meaningful assemblage of materials, ideals, and trajectories of potential experiences (Figure 5.1). Packing might be a well-rehearsed routine that frequent travellers undertake with relative ease and efficiency. Or it might be the first time packing; it might be a different set of material objects that have been packed together, or there could be climatic influences that we respond to, such as wind, rain, or cold that we are packing in (see Barry 2017). The key here is the ability to recall past experiences of packing as a practice that

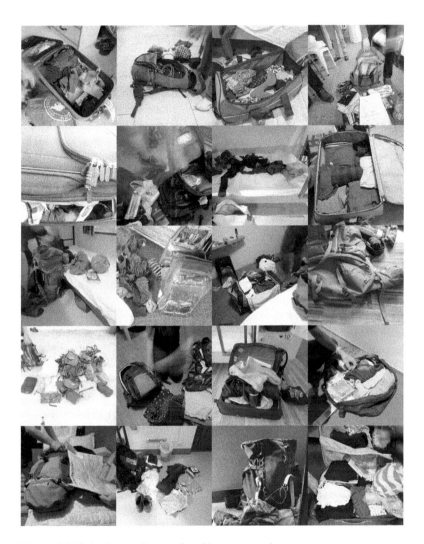

Figure 5.1 Multiple experiences of packing as a practice

is continually adapted and adjusted to each new situation. This involves prepending our mobile relations across various spatio-temporal registers (past packing, future travel, and the present assemblage of actors). It is the stirring of relations, which are recalled from past experiences, our kinetic knowledges, and our imaginative capacity, that together become the 'event-in-the-making' (Manning 2013, p. 7). It is an accumulation of experience, sensation, and movement that informs and unfolds a relationship between subject-object and experience.

Attention to materiality becomes a way to intensify the examination into the collective practices that unfold through tourism mobilities. I have approached materiality through not just a metaphor but as a practical and theoretical imperative, because it gives prominence to the materially driven interactions. An emphasis on the materiality of tourist practices implies that materials (which constitute our bodies, objects, architectures, and landscapes) are in constant negotiation as we configure ourselves with each inter-action (see Chapter 2). Practices that harness the materiality of the situation, or that embrace the flux, flows, and fluidity of communal movements, are central to further examinations of how tourist actions contribute to global mobilities in various capacities. The knowledges that are gained from interacting with materials—such as tactile, kinetic, and collaborative experiences—emphasise the overlaps between touristic situations and everyday life, where the materials we interact with enable and support our habits and routines. This is a practice-led approach that reveals the methodological and ontological concerns in mobilities that value alternative, inclusive, and creative practices.

Knowledge and creativity are by no means fixed; rather, they are fluid and relational (much like materiality) and are key to forming part of the heterogeneous qualities of the way we navigate each encounter. My understanding of creative knowledge production and transmission arises from creative arts and humanities research where practice and theory are inseparable (Barrett and Bolt 2007; Bolt 2004; Carter 2004). Creative and processual practices value engagement, interaction, and the 'hands-on' approaches (Barry 2016) that tourists are already in the midst of. Tourists are already feeling, sensing, and responding in tactile and corporeal ways. The actions they do (whether in packing or other daily tasks) are embodied practices that reflect creative encounters with materials (see Chapter 2; Franklin 2014; Haldrup and Larsen 2010; Urry and Larsen 2011). In this sense, creative forms of knowledge production provide insights into the possibilities of everyday practices in terms of how they situate, register, and respond to the array of actors they are in motion with.

It is imperative that we take materiality seriously because it connects us (humans) to the global concerns of how we move collectively, and the environmental constraints and consumption that tourism movements produce. Nigel Thrift reminds us that 'increasingly what counts as "we" is being redefined by a range of transhuman' encounters (2007, p. 17). Human action is never isolated, and, particularly in tourism, is always supported by an array of nonhuman material actors. In this manner, the 'stuff' that we bring with us in our bags, that we travel with, becomes an important indicator of how, where, and why tourists move. For mobilities and tourism researchers, understanding and valuing the role that materiality plays in shaping tourist practices (whether in the interactions with an object or the material co-constitution of an environment) is vital in how we assess consumption patterns, expectations, and ideals, or the possibilities for alternative forms of tourism experiences.

Moments when tourists experience practices that aid in situating oneself, or that help gain bearings in the surroundings, have the potential to affect us in unanticipated ways. To practice means to be responsive to the 'intricate web of interrelations' that position us within an environment (Braidotti 2012a, p. 173). Letting yourself 'drift' while doing an everyday routine might mean that you indulge in familiarity, comfort, or the sensations that situate you in the environment. These are moments where practices are integral in our lives, establishing our bearings and allowing us to experience 'being right where you are', attuning to the movements in the moment, but 'more intensely' (Massumi 2015, p. 3). Practices that guide our routines and movements are also intensely relational, responding to the flux of sensory and kinetic registers.

A relational approach to practice relies on the ability of learning 'to reinvent oneself, and [how] one desires the self as a process of transformation' (Braidotti 2012b, p. 41). Action is never isolated to the individual but acknowledges that we are bound within an assemblage of actors operating at different speeds, intensities, and material and spatial boundaries. Moments when we are open to sensations that are beyond the immediacy of our own expectations offer transversal experiences[1] that are 'ultimately collective' (Braidotti 2012b, p. 43). And seeing as tourism frequently relies on situations where we seek out overwhelming or astounding experiences, where we want to be disoriented by the resonances of the destinations that we travel to (see Chapter 4), then transversal experiences might be one way to further examine more sustainable and inclusive tourist practices (Barry 2017). In this way, tourists are already primed for alternative modes of experience that force us to adjust practices and (re)compose in new and unfamiliar situations.

Of course, this can be difficult, and is not always possible. To be clear, I am not suggesting that each and every tourist reposition themselves as open and adaptable to every movement and every change. There is room, and necessity, for attention to individual intentions and desires that navigate our touristic ideals and journeys. However, there is also room for change in tourist practices and the manner in which the role of touristic ideals and experiences is understood. This requires attention to interactions with materials, the spatial and environmental ideals that guide our journeys, and how practices of mobilities present challenges and changes that 'involve novel, extensive and "flickering" combinations of the presence and absence' (Urry 2016, p. 16). To this end, a nomadic approach which values interaction across differences (Braidotti 2012b), from macro to micro, human and non-human, and is inclusive of local and 'transnational and planetary mobilities' (Sheller and Urry 2016, p. 21), offers fresh perspectives on the practices that many mobile subjects are already doing.

Packing for Future Mobile Scenarios

Packing a bag accentuates the complexity involved in everyday mobilities practices, yet connects us to global tourist ideals. It is a practice that blurs everyday actions, global concerns, and individual ideals and desires. Examples of how tourists practice mobilities can be found in the obvious touristic activities (such as tours, exploration, sightseeing), but as I have shown, these practices are also felt in smaller, mundane activities (packing, washing, cooking, and so on). It is this shift across habitual routines and spontaneous interactions that encourages creative and collaborative modes of knowing and practicing. These might develop in the routine, mundane actions that we undertake (Crouch 2003; Ehn and Lofgren 2010; Edensor 2007; Pink 2012), where we feel ourselves 'drift'. Or, practices might develop in instances where we feel overwhelmed or disoriented by the situation (Anderson 2015; Sverrisdóttir 2011) and astounded by the aesthetics of our surrounds (Benediktsson and Lund 2010; Huijbens and Benediktsson 2013; Lund 2013). Or, it might just be in the moments when we are playfully going with the flow in unexpected encounters (Sheller and Urry 2004; see Chapter 4). These adaptive and generative capacities resonate through tourist activities and frequently rely on valuing, trusting, and inviting other modes of knowing.

Actions that constitute 'everyday' mobilities practices can traverse a range of situations, sites, and experiences; they are not necessarily isolated to one particular location or application (de Certeau 1984, p. 29). For instance, the process of re-orientation or adjustment of routines that is experienced in a certain tourist destination might be reproduced or adapted at a later instance in another place. The 'modalities of action' (de Certeau 1984, p. 29), that is, the techniques used to gauge our experience, situate ourselves, and adjust to the surroundings, can traverse leisure and tourism, everyday banal moments, or be applied in later practices of creativity, research, or expression.

Rethinking mobilities practices as collaborative processes has implications for how future tourism and mobilities research is conducted. The relationship between material interactions and the belongings we bring with us (how and what we consume, discard, or share) is one avenue to consider and evaluate the impact of tourism. Because tourists are always in flux, movements are always traversing practical applications and idealised conceptions of what we think we should be doing and experiencing. The infamous Lonely Planet guide to packing advises that 'the liberation of decluttering is magical. Travel light, learn to simply "be"' (Lonely Planet 2016, p. 34). Travelling 'light' might be the ideal, but we all know that the reality of packing a bag is much messier and entangled. Packing brings to the forefront the material concerns of how tourists interact, consume, discard, and co-produce experiences and practices of mobilities. Materiality, in this vein, is key to understanding the creative and processual knowledges that are produced.

The expectations of environmental encounters, particularly of vast and unique landscape areas, need to be carefully considered in terms of how tourist imaginaries are cultivated through material, aesthetic, and multi-sensory registers. Understanding the environment as intrinsically bound to the human and nonhuman, material and immaterial actors that are moving together is central to further investigations of how mobilities play a role in co-consumptive and co-productive practices. For tourist destinations, there are concerns of matching touristic expectations and idealised imagery, particularly of landscapes and natural areas, which are being visited by increasing tourist numbers each year. Attention to the relational experiences that tourists have (Benediktsson and Lund 2010; Lund 2013), and the recognition that the environment is a collective experience of a particular place, is one possibility for reconceptualising tourist expectations. For instance, how do increasing numbers of tourists accept and accommodate the fact that previously off-the-beaten-track destinations, such as rural Iceland, are now filling with tour busses and crowds? Finding ways to acknowledge that tourism—whether guided tours or solo backpacking trips—feeds into global flows and that individual expectations need to be adjusted is an issue that needs further scrutiny.

Similarly, research into tourism to environmental and 'wilderness' areas, such as National Parks and World Heritage areas, shows the concern of what tourists expect their experience to be and the reality of their visit in terms of impact and satisfaction (Dorwart, Moore and Leung 2009; Pietilä and Fagerholm 2016; Wearing and Whenman 2009). Frequently, the travel to environmental destinations involves the expectation of pristine and untouched 'nature', void of any other human presence or traces of anthropogenic influences (Franklin 2006; Palsson 2013). In these situations, the materials that tourists bring with them—what they pack in their bags—is highly dependent on the material constitution and capacity to enable durational tourist experiences (Michael 2000; Walsh and Tucker 2009). Indeed, in terms of packing for durational walks, treks, camping, or other 'outdoor' leisure activities, there are often vastly different expectations of the facilities provided and what space humans need to share in order to co-habit with each other. To this end, I have proposed that alternative practices of tourism mobilities draw attention to the affirmative and affective resonances that occur every day in tourism. Valuing the micro, minute, mundane moments where we are already open to other influences and sensations offers new ways of understanding and thinking about the impact of our practices and mobilities begin to surface.

Conclusion

The examples that have been examined in this book indicate a range of procedures that overlap with and extend on everyday practices of mobilities. Daily processes of moving and being in transition encompass interactions with an array of actors as we creatively negotiate the unfolding of material and spatial complexities. If only momentarily, our movements are open to the potential of collective action. When we collaborate and attune to the subtleties of experience that are often beyond individual actions, we create opportunities for new creative practices and modes of experience that enrich our lives, clarify our interactions, and impact on the environments we are with/in.

Situations emerge where our bodily and material constitution are drawn into an ecology of human and nonhuman action. By expanding on moments where touristic ideals mesh with sensation, the potential for collaborative experiences that breach anthropocentric orientation arise. Moments when our daily routines contrast with what we think we are supposed to feel or achieve reveal opportunities for re-composing oneself in relation to alternative forms of encounter. These are practices of mobilities that involve collaborative and materially driven interactions with an array of human and nonhuman actors. Consequently, these situations infuse with everyday *and* touristic actions in collective processes and signal new modalities of experiencing mobility.

There is need for further flexibility in understanding how knowledge is produced through movement, and many researchers are calling for new approaches and techniques to studying mobilities practices (Adey, Bissel, Hannam, Merriman and Sheller 2014; Barry and Keane 2017; Coles, Hall and Duval 2009, p. 92; Hui 2013; Urry 2016; Witzgall, Vogl and Kesselring 2013). Teasing out the relations between tourists, practices, and materials (human and nonhuman) takes into account alternative and process-based investigations. As I have shown in this book, new knowledge on how tourists move, what they move with, and how these movements are collaborative co-consumption experiences is achieved through inquiries into points where movement, action, and the boundaries of individuals and the collective meet. To this end, a focus on knowledge production that values creative, collaborative, and materially driven interactions warrants reflexive and postdisciplinary understandings of movement and mobilities.

Practices of tourism mobilities are evident in a range of situations where individualised and collective movements are blurred. This fusion of actors and agencies occurs on macro and micro scales and requires adaptive and transformative nomadic abilities to situate ourselves in the collective flows of the global. The breadth of tourism mobilities needs to be carefully considered in relation to increasing human and nonhuman movements around the Earth. The drastic impacts on planetary systems, local and global tourism and migration cultures, and individual capacities or national restrictions on movement necessitate alternative and creative modes of mobility. A call for collective action where mobilities are understood across a range of scales, actors, and practices should be encouraged.

Note

1 Transversality is understood as the experience 'where we feel entangled and aware of how we shift and move' with others (Barry 2017, p. 2). To practice transversally is to shift and craft relationships that affirm and include multiple perspectives (Braidotti 2013; Rhoades and Brunner 2010). Transversality is the capacity to be open to a myriad of encounters that forge 'connections among material and symbolic, concrete and discursive, lines and forces' (Braidotti 2012a, p. 171). In this sense, transversal moments are integrally bound to material practices that form through interactions with an array of actors.

References

Adey, P., Bissel, D., Hannam, K., Merriman, P. and Sheller, M. eds. 2014. *The Routledge handbook of mobilities*. New York: Routledge.

Anderson, J. 2015. 'Exploring the consequences of mobility: Reclaiming jet lag as the state of travel disorientation', *Mobilities*, vol. 10, no. 1, pp. 1–16. doi:10.1080/17450101.2013.806392

Barrett, E. and Bolt, B. 2007. *Practice as research: Approaches to creative arts enquiry*. London: I.B. Tauris.

Barry, K. 2015. 'The aesthetics of aircraft safety cards: Spatial negotiations and affective mobilities in diagrammatic instructions', *Mobilities*, first published online before Print: 2 Nov, 2015. doi:10.1080/17450101.2015.1086101

Barry, K. 2016. 'Diagramming: A creative methodology for tourist studies', *Tourist Studies*. First published online before print: Nov 28, 2016. doi:10.1177/1468797616680852

Barry, K. 2017. 'Transversal travels: The relational movements and environmental intensities of packing a bag', *Studies in Material Thinking*, vol. 16, pp. 1–17.

Barry, K. and Keane, J. 2017. 'Moving within mobilities: Expanding spatial experiences through the artwork PAN & ZOOM', *Applied Mobilities*, vol. 2, no. 1, pp. 67–84. doi:10.1080/23800127.2016.1272971

Benediktsson, K. and Lund, K.A. eds. 2010. *Conversations with landscape*. Farnham: Ashgate.

Bennett, J. 2010. *Vibrant matter: A political ecology of things*. Durham: Duke University Press.

Bissel, D. and Fuller, G. eds. 2011. *Stillness in a mobile world*. Oxon and New York: Routledge.

Bissell, D. 2009. 'Inconsequential materialities: The movements of lost effects', *Space and Culture*, vol. 12, no. 1, pp. 95–115. doi:10.1177/1206331208325602

Bolt, B. 2004. *Art beyond representation: The performative power of the image*. London and New York: I.B. Taurus.

Braidotti, R. 2012a. 'Afterword', *Angelaki: Journal of the Theoretical Humanities*, vol. 17, no. 2, pp. 169–176. doi:10.1080/0969725X.2012.701056

Braidotti, R. 2012b. *Nomadic theory: The portable Rosi Braidotti*. New York: Columbia University Press.

Braidotti, R. 2013. *The posthuman*. Cambridge and Malden, MA: Polity Press.

Braidotti, R. 2016. 'Rosi Braidotti: DON'T AGONIZE, ORGANIZE!', *E-flux*. Retrieved 15 November 2016, from: http://conversations.e-flux.com/t/rosi-braidotti-don-t-agonize-organize/5294

Carter, P. 2004. *Material thinking: The theory and practice of creative research*. Carlton, VIC: Melbourne University Press.

Channel 4 News. 2016. 'This is why refugees have smartphones—Hala's story', *YouTube*. Retrieved 23 January 2017 from: www.youtube.com/watch?v=gc_5 ksnkGA0

Clark, N. and Hird, M.J. 2014. 'Deep shit', *O-Zone: A Journal of Object-Oriented Studies*, vol. 1, no. 1, pp. 44–52.

Coles, T., Hall, M.C. and Duval, D.T. 2009. 'Post-disciplinary tourism'. *In*: J. Tribe, ed. *Philosophical issues in tourism*. Bristol: Channel View Publications, pp. 80–100.

Crouch, D. 2003. 'Spacing, performing, and becoming: Tangles in the mundane', *Environment and Planning A*, vol. 35, no. 11, pp. 1945–1960. doi:10.1068/a3585

de Certeau, M. 1984. *The practice of everyday life*. London: University of California Press.

Dorwart, C.E., Moore, R.L., and Leung, Y. 2009. 'Visitors' perceptions of a trail environment and effects on experiences: A model for nature-based recreation experiences', *Leisure Sciences*, vol. 32, no. 1, pp. 33–53. doi:10.1080/01490400903430863

Edensor, T. 2007. 'Mundane mobilities, performances and spaces of tourism', *Social & Cultural Geography*, vol. 8, no. 2, pp. 799–215. doi:10.1080/14649360701360089

Ehn, B. and Lofgren, O. 2010. 'Doing an ethnography of "non-events"'. *In: The secret world of doing nothing*. Berkeley, Los Angeles and London: University of California Press, pp. 217–241.

Franklin, A. 2006. 'The humanity of wilderness photography?', *Australian Humanities Review*, vol. 38, pp. 1–16. Retrieved 14 March 2017, from: http://australian humanitiesreview.org/2006/04/01/the-humanity-of-wilderness-photography/

Franklin, A. 2014. 'On why we dig the beach: Tracing the subjects and objects of the bucket and spade for a relational materialist theory of the beach' *Tourist Studies*, vol. 14, no. 3, pp. 261–285. doi:10.177/1468797614536331.

Gren, M. and Huijbens, E.H. 2012. 'Tourism theory and the earth', *Annals of Tourism Research*, vol. 39, no. 1, pp. 155–170. doi:10.1016/j.annals.2011.05.009

Gren, M. and Huijbens, E.H. 2014. 'Tourism and the anthropocene', *Scandinavian Journal of Hospitality and Tourism*, vol. 14, no. 1, pp. 6–22. doi:10.1080/15022 250.2014.886100

Haldrup, M. and Larsen, J. 2010. *Tourism, performance, and the everyday: Consuming the orient*. Oxon and New York: Routledge.

Hui, A. 2013. 'Moving with practices: The discontinuous, rhythmic and material mobilities of leisure', *Social & Cultural Geography*, vol. 14, no. 8, pp. 888–908. doi:10.1080/14649365.2013.827736

Huijbens, E. and Benediktsson, K. 2013. 'Inspiring the visitor? Landscapes and horizons of hospitality', *Tourist Studies*, vol. 13, no. 2, pp. 189–208. doi:10.1177/ 146879613490378

International Refugee Committee. 2015. 'What's in my bag? What refugees bring when they run for their lives', *Medium*. Retrieved 23 January 2017 from: https:// medium.com/uprooted/what-s-in-my-bag-758d435f6e62#.uxdo63l78

Latour, B. 2004. *Politics of nature: How to bring the sciences into democracy*. Cambridge, MA and London: Harvard University Press.

Latour, B. 2014. 'Agency at the time of the anthropocene', *New Literary History*, vol. 45, no. 1, pp. 1–18. doi:10.1353/nlh.2014.0003

Lonely Planet. 2016. *How to pack for any trip*. Carlton: Lonely Planet Publications Pty Ltd.

Lund, K.A. 2013. 'Experiencing nature in nature-based tourism', *Tourist Studies*, vol. 13, no. 2, pp. 156–171. doi:10.1177/1468797613490373

Manning, E. 2013. *Always more than one*. Durham, NC: Duke University Press.

Massumi, B. 2015. *Politics of affect*. Cambridge: Polity.

Merriman, P. 2016. 'Mobilities II: Cruising', *Progress in Human Geography*, vol. 40, no. 4, pp. 555–564. doi:10.1177/0309132515585654

Merriman, P., Revill, G., Cresswell, T., Lorimer, H., Matless, D., Rose, G. and Wylie, J. 2008. 'Landscape, mobility, practice', *Social & Cultural Geography*, vol. 9, no. 2, pp. 191–212.

Michael, M. 2000. 'These boots are made for walking . . .: Mundane technology, the body and human-environment relations', *Body and Society*, vol. 6, no. 3–4, pp. 107–126.

Mol, A. and Law, J. 1994. 'Regions, networks and fluids: Anaemia and social topology', *Social Studies of Science*, vol. 24, no. 4, pp. 641–671. doi:10.1177/ 030631279402400402

Morton, T. 2013. *Hyperobjects: Philosophy and ecology after the end of the world*. Minneapolis and London: University of Minnesota Press.

Palsson, G. 2013. 'Ensembles of biosocial relations'. *In*: T. Ingold and G. Palsson, eds. *Biosocial becomings: Integrating social and biological anthropology*. New York: Cambridge University Press, pp. 22–41.

Palsson, G., Szerszynski, B., Sörlin, S., Marks, J., Avril, B., Crumley, C., Hackmann, H., Holm, P., Ingram, J., Kirman, A., Buendía, M.P. and Weekhuizen, R. 2013. 'Reconceptualizing the "Anthropos" in the Anthropocene: Integrating the social sciences and humanities in global environmental change research', *Environmental Science and Policy*, vol. 28, pp. 3–13. doi:10.1016/j.envsci.2012. 11.004

Pietilä, M. and Fagerholm, N. 2016. 'Visitors' place-based evaluations of unacceptable tourism impacts in Oulanka National Park, Finland', *Tourism Geographies*, vol. 18, no. 3, pp. 258–279. doi:10.1080/14616688.2016.1169313

Pink, S. 2012. *Situating everyday life: Practices and places*. London: Sage.

Ram, A. 2015. 'Smartphones bring solace and aid to desperate refugees', *Wired*. Retrieved 23 January 2017 from: www.wired.com/2015/12/smartphone-syrian-refugee-crisis/

Ren, C. Jóhannesson, G.T. and Van der Duim, R. 2012. 'How ANT works'. *In*: R. Van der Duim, C. Ren and G.T. Jóhannesson, eds. *Actor-network theory and tourism: Ordering, materiality and multiplicity*. Oxon: Routledge, pp. 13–25.

Rhoades, T. and Brunner, C. 2010. 'Transversal fields of experience', *Inflexions*, vol. 4, pp. i–viii. Retrieved 14 March 2017, from: www.inflexions.org/n4_intro html.html

Richards, G. and Wilson, J. eds. 2004. 'Drifting towards the global nomad'. *In: The global nomad: Backpacker travel in theory and practice*. Channel View Publications, pp. 3–13.

Sheller, M. and Urry, J. eds. 2004. 'Places to play, places in play'. *In: Tourism mobilities: Places to play, places in play*. London: Routledge, pp. 1–10.

Sheller, M. and Urry, J. 2016. 'Mobilizing the new mobilities paradigm', *Applied Mobilities*, vol. 1, no. 1, pp. 10–25. doi:10.1080/23800127.2016.1151216

Sverrisdóttir, H. 2011. 'The destination within', *Journal of the Association of Icelandic Geographers/Landabréfið*, vol. 25, pp. 77–84.

Thrift, N. 2007. *Non-representational theory: Space, politics, affect*. London: Routledge.

UNHCR. 2015. *Global trends: Forced displacement in 2015*. Retrieved 16 February 2017 from: www.unhcr.org/576408cd7.pdf

UNWTO. 2016. *Tourism highlights, 2016 edition*. Retrieved 3 February 2017, from: www.e-unwto.org/doi/pdf/10.18111/9789284418145

Urry, J. 2003. *Global complexity*. Malden, MA: Polity Press.

Urry, J. 2011. 'Does mobility have a future?'. *In*: M. Grieco and J. Urry, eds. *Mobilities: New perspectives on transport and society*. Farnham: Ashgate, pp. 3–20.

Urry, J. 2014. *Offshoring*. Cambridge: Polity Press.

Urry, J. 2016. *Mobilities*. Cambridge: Polity Press.

Urry, J. and Larsen, J. 2011. *The tourist gaze 3.0*. London: Sage Publication Ltd.

Van der Duim, R., Ren, C. and Jóhannesson, G.T. eds. 2012. *Actor-network theory and tourism: Ordering, materiality and multiplicity*. Oxon: Routledge.

Veijola, S., Molz, J.G., Pyyhtinen, O., Höckert, E. and Grit, A. eds. 2014. 'Introduction: Alternative tourism ontologies'. *In: Disruptive tourism and its untidy guests*. Hampshire and New York: Palgrave Macmillan, pp. 1–18.

Walsh, N. and Tucker, H. 2009. 'Tourism "things": The travelling performance of the backpack', *Tourist Studies*, vol. 9, no. 3, pp. 223–239. doi:10.1177/14687 97610382706

Wearing, S. and Whenman, A. 2009. 'Tourism as an interpretive and mediating influence: A review of the authority of guidebooks in protected areas', *Tourism Analysis*, vol. 14, no. 5, pp. 701–716.

Witzgall, S., Vogl, G. and Kesselring, S. eds. 2013. *New mobilities regimes in art and social sciences*. Farnham: Ashgate.

Index